LIVING PLANET

Camilla de la Bédoyère

W
WELBECK

THIS IS A WELBECK CHILDREN'S BOOK

Text, design and illustration
© Welbeck Children's Limited 2020

Published in 2020 by Welbeck Children's Limited
An imprint of the Welbeck Publishing Group
20 Mortimer Street, London W1T 3JW

ISBN: 978-1-78312-529-6

All rights reserved. This book is sold subject to the condition that it may not be reproduced, stored in a retrieval system or transmitted in any form or by any means, electronic, mechanical, photocopying, recording or otherwise, without the publisher's prior consent.

A catalogue record for this book is available from the British Library.

Designer: Ceri Hurst
Design Manager: Emily Clarke
Editor: Jenni Lazell
Picture Research: Paul Langan
Production: Nicola Davey

Printed in Heshan, China

987654321

Picture credits:

The publishers would like to thank the following sources for their kind permission to reproduce the pictures and footage in this book. The numbers listed below give the page on which they appear in the book.

(T=top, B=bottom, L=left, R=right, C=centre, UP=upper, LOW=lower)

ALAMY: /ClipDealer GmbH: 27C **GETTY IMAGES:** /Yuri Arcurs: 8; /Dave Einsel: 84; /Visual China Group: 19T **PETER LIDDIARD:** 12, 16–17, 22, 68–69, 80 **NATURE PICTURE LIBRARY:** /John Abbott: 47B; /Aflo: 6–7; /Neil Aldridge: 55R; /Bryan & Cherry Alexander: 85B; /Ingo Arndt: 72–73; /Eric Baccega: 75B; /Espen Bergersen: 90B; /Will Burrard-Lucas: 6; /Adam Burton: 65B; /Mark Carwardine: 51B; /Jordi Chias: 90–91; /Claudio Contreras: 93T; /Ashley Cooper: 26B; /Russell Cooper: 25CL; /Sylvain Cordier: 89B; /Christophe Courteau: 77T, 92–93; /Stephen Dalton: 56B; /Tui De Roy: 23C, 50B; /Oscar Dewhurst: 25R; /Andres M Dominguez: 39T; /Rob Drummond/BIA: 76L; /Jack Dykinga: 9B, 14–15, 38–39; /Klaus Echle: 65T; /Guy Edwardes: 21B, 42C; /Gerry Ellis: 54T; /Suzi Eszterhas: 59C; /Chris & Monique Fallows: 48–49; /Michael & Patricia Fogden: 35B, 51C, 56–57; /Jeff Foott: 66–67; /Jurgen Freund: 46T, 48B; /David Gallan: 33B, 58T; /Nick Garbutt: 70T, 70B; /Sergey Gorshkov: 64T; /Danny Green: 64B; /Shane Gross: 79T; /Orsolya Haarberg: 9C; /Graham Hatherley: 37B; /Tony Heald: 58B; /Oliver Hellowell: 55L; /Daniel Heuclin: 32B; /Paul Hobson: 57B; /Sam Hobson: 87B; /Ross Hoddinott: 9T, 39C; /Michael Hutchinson: 11T; /Alex Hyde: 37T, 45T; /Jabruson Motion: 92B; /Ernie Janes: 43T; /Sandesh Kadur: 73T; /Olga Kamenskaya: 75T; /Steven Kazlowski: 62–63; /Klein & Hubert: 3, 25CR, 45B, 51T, 55B, 60–61, 63T; /Rhonda Klevansky: 24B; /Chien Lee: 44–45, 88B; /Enrique Lopez-Tapia: 23T; /Alastair MacEwen: 43B; /Luiz Claudio Marigo: 67T; /Luke Massey: 87T; /Eric Medard: 54C; /Claus Meyer: 74B; /Hiroya Minakuchi: 53C; /Yva Momatiuk & John Eastcott: 62T; /Colin Monteath: 14B, 76–77; /Vincent Munier: 41T; /Juan Carlos Munoz: 32T, 38L, 53B; /Alex Mustard: 18–19, 20–21, 49B, 81T; /Nature Production: 43C; /Ramon Navarro: 2; /Chris Newbert: 47TL; /David Noton: 88T; /Rolf Nussbaumer: 77B; /Fred Olivier: 62B; /David Perpinan: 52B; /Doug Perrine: 10R; /Inaki Relanzon: 78–79; /Michel Roggo: 15B, 37C, 74T; /Andy Rouse: 16B, 35T, 56T, 70–71; /Jose B Ruiz: 59T; /Cyril Ruoso: 27B, 54B; /Andy Sands: 41B; /Scotland: The Big Picture: 46B; /Anup Shah: 28–29, 34–35; /David Shale: 18B, 81C, 81C LOW 81B; /Sinclair Stammers: 47TR; /Paul D Stewart: 35C, 85T; /Lynn M Stone: 72B; /Charlie Summers: 59B; /Kim Taylor: 36B; /Steve O Taylor: 66B; /David Tipling: 81C UP; /Floris van Breugel: 73B; /Wim van den Heever: 1, 69C; /Markus Varesvuo: 25L; /Visuals Unlimited: 26–27, 30–31, 36T, 50T, 53T; /Gerrit Vyn: 19B; /Staffan Widstrand/Wild Wonders of China: 89T; /Wild Wonders of Europe/Lesniewski: 52–53; /Wild Wonders of Europe/Pitkin: 79B; /Wild Wonders of Europe/Zankl: 92T; /Mike Wilkes: 15T; /Paul Williams: 24–25; /David Woodfall: 75C; /Konrad Wothe: 47C; /Tony Wu: 55T; /Solvin Zankl: 42–43 **SHUTTERSTOCK:** /BlueRingMedia: 40T; /Ryan M Bolton: 78B; /Designua: 10B, 18T, 20B; /Thomas Dutour: 13B; /eveleen: 40B; /Flystock: 21T; /guentermanaus: 69T; /industryviews: 86B; /Petr Klabal: 69B; /Ivan Kurmyshov: 86–87; /NicoElNino: 82–83; /solarseven: 4–5; /Rashevskyi Viacheslav: 11B; /vitstudio: 34T; /Wead: 13C

Every effort has been made to acknowledge correctly and contact the source and/or copyright holder of each picture, any unintentional errors or omissions will be corrected in future editions of this book.

HOW TO ACCESS AUGMENTED REALITY FEATURES

1 Go to the Google Play Store or the Apple App Store and download the FREE Living Planet app.

2 Some pages in the book have augmented reality features. Look out for the boxes marked with a play symbol for videos.

3 View the page through the app to watch full-motion video on the page!

CONTENTS

4 THE BIRTH OF A LIVING PLANET

- 6 The Birth of Earth
- 8 The Structure of Earth
- 10 On the Move
- 12 Fire and Fury
- 14 Dynamic Earth
- 16 Water
- 18 The World Ocean
- 20 Active Oceans
- 22 The Atmosphere
- 24 Climate and Weather
- 26 Extreme Weather

28 WONDER OF LIFE

- 30 Life Begins
- 32 Prehistoric Life
- 34 Evolution and Extinction
- 36 Kingdoms of Life
- 38 Plant Life
- 40 How Plants Live
- 42 Flowers and Seeds
- 44 Fungi
- 46 Invertebrate Life
- 48 Vertebrate Life
- 50 Reptiles and Amphibians
- 52 Birds
- 54 Mammals
- 56 How Animals Live
- 58 Life Cycles

60 HABITATS

- 62 The Polar Biome
- 64 Temperate Forests
- 66 Grasslands
- 68 Tropical Rainforests
- 70 Tropical Dry Forests
- 72 Mountains
- 74 Rivers and Wetlands
- 76 Coasts
- 78 Shallow Water
- 80 Open Oceans

82 PEOPLE AND THE PLANET

- 84 The First Humans
- 86 Human Habitats
- 88 Feeding the World
- 90 Changing the Planet
- 92 Looking Ahead

- 94 Glossary
- 96 Index

1 THE BIRTH OF A LIVING PLANET

THE STORY OF OUR PRECIOUS BLUE PLANET BEGAN WHEN THE UNIVERSE WAS CREATED, ABOUT 14 BILLION YEARS AGO. At first, Earth was a hot, dry and rocky place where nothing could live. Over time it changed into a unique place that had all the ingredients needed to support life, which probably began at least 3.8 billion years ago. The very first living things were tiny and simple, but since then life has evolved into the enormous range of complex animals and plants that we share our beautiful planet with today.

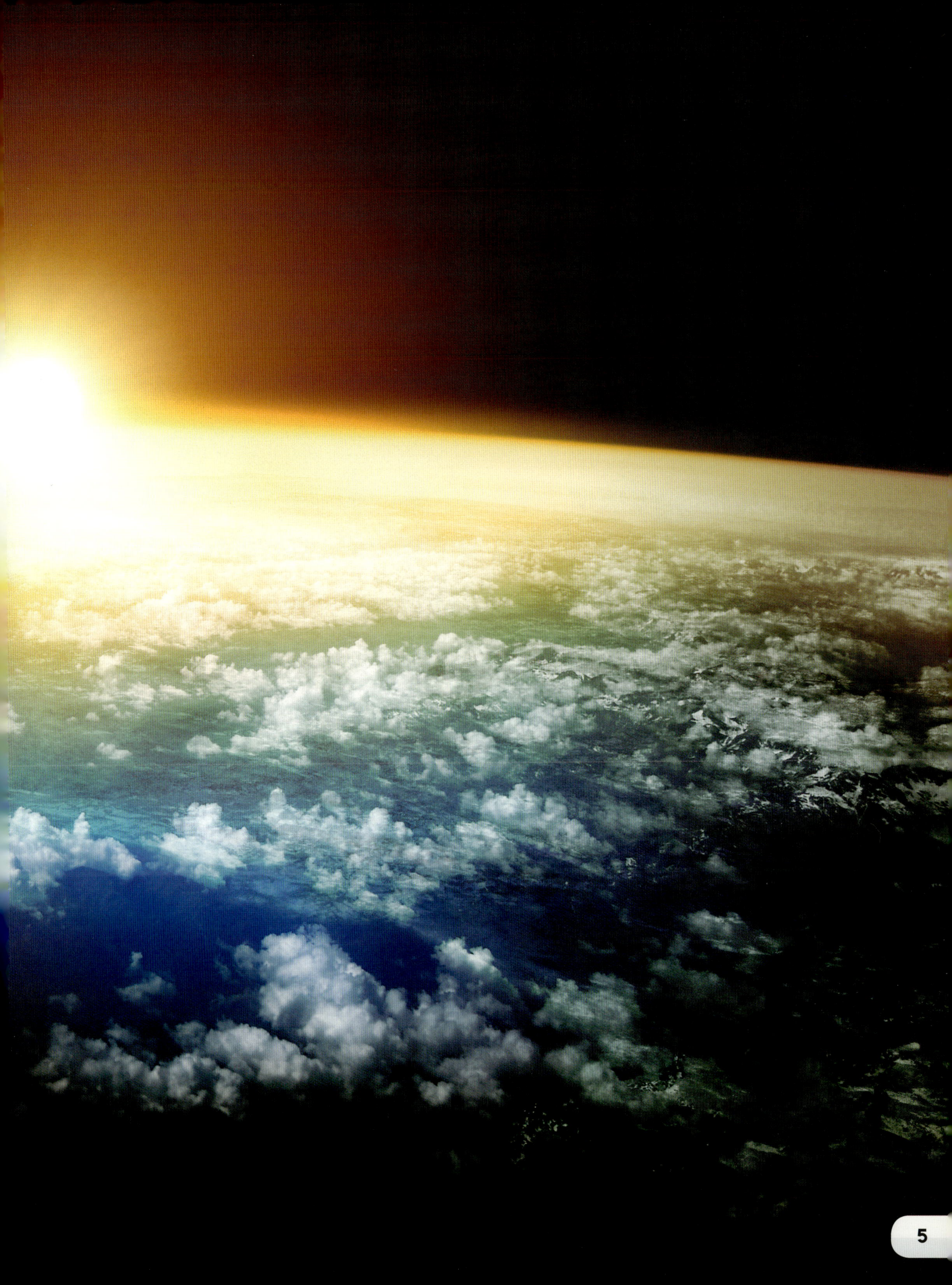

THE BIRTH OF EARTH

THE UNIVERSE PROBABLY BEGAN 13.7 BILLION YEARS AGO, when energy and light mixed with tiny particles that would one day become all the planets and stars. Suddenly, all the particles began to stretch out, or expand, at a point in time called the Big Bang. As the particles spread out they cooled down and began to collect as spinning clouds of dust and gas, and eventually they collapsed to form stars, planets and moons. Our Sun was formed this way less than five billion years ago.

THE SOLAR SYSTEM

The Sun is the star at the centre of our solar system. Eight planets, including Earth, orbit this burning ball of gases. The Sun releases energy as it burns, and this energy gives us heat and light – without the Sun there would be no life on Earth.

There are also five dwarf planets, around 190 moons and thousands of comets and asteroids that travel with the planets around our star. The solar system is one of many similar collections of suns and planets that exist together in a galaxy called the Milky Way.

THE SUN

The Sun is mostly made of the gases hydrogen and helium. As it burns, the Sun turns hydrogen into helium and releases vast amounts of energy. We experience some of that energy as heat and light here on Earth. One day, the Sun will run out of fuel to burn and then it will turn into a red giant, which is a larger, cooler type of star that is dying. Thankfully, that won't happen for another five billion years!

THE THIRD PLANET

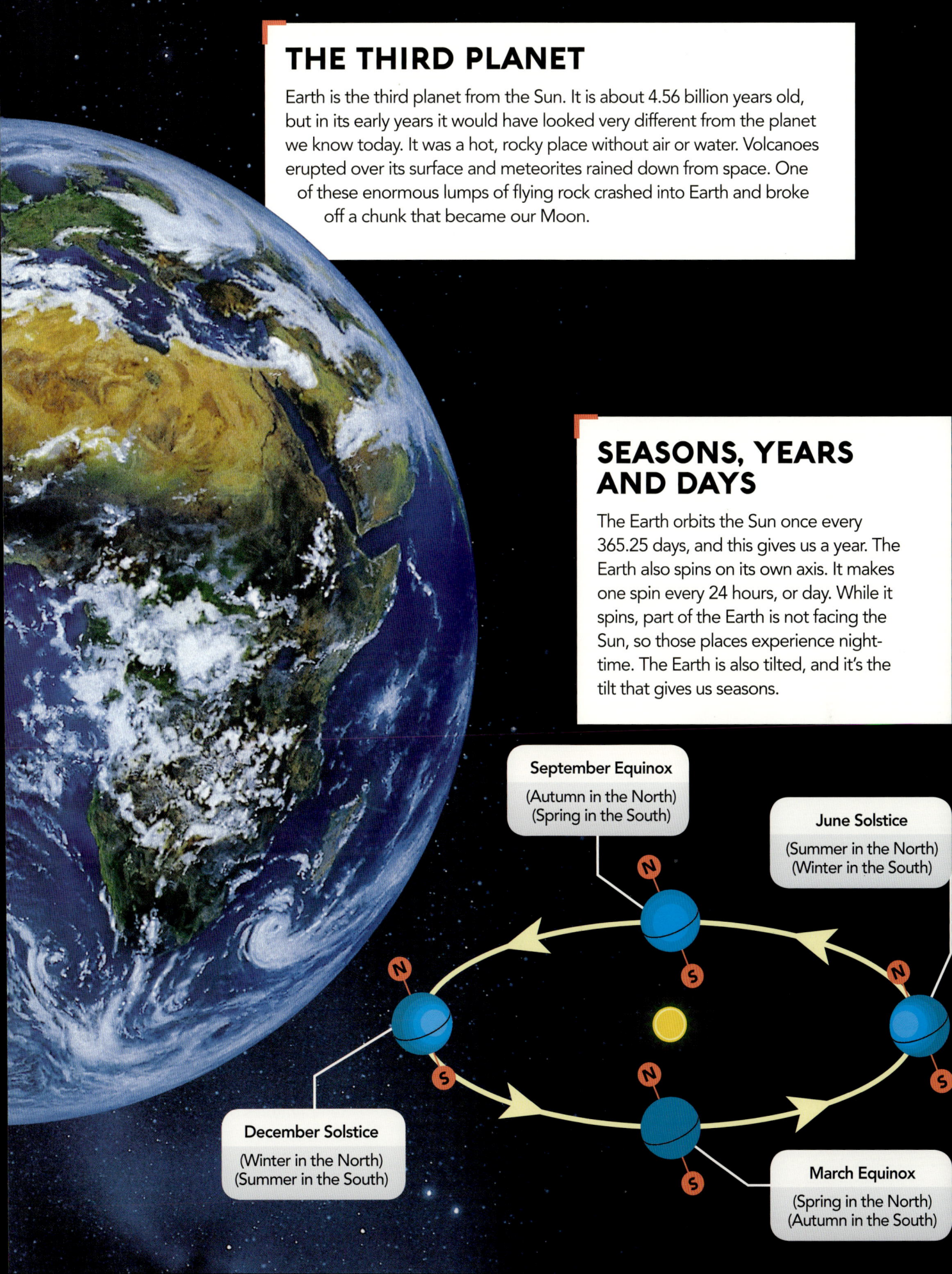

Earth is the third planet from the Sun. It is about 4.56 billion years old, but in its early years it would have looked very different from the planet we know today. It was a hot, rocky place without air or water. Volcanoes erupted over its surface and meteorites rained down from space. One of these enormous lumps of flying rock crashed into Earth and broke off a chunk that became our Moon.

SEASONS, YEARS AND DAYS

The Earth orbits the Sun once every 365.25 days, and this gives us a year. The Earth also spins on its own axis. It makes one spin every 24 hours, or day. While it spins, part of the Earth is not facing the Sun, so those places experience night-time. The Earth is also tilted, and it's the tilt that gives us seasons.

September Equinox
(Autumn in the North)
(Spring in the South)

June Solstice
(Summer in the North)
(Winter in the South)

December Solstice
(Winter in the North)
(Summer in the South)

March Equinox
(Spring in the North)
(Autumn in the South)

THE STRUCTURE OF EARTH

EARTH IS A ROCKY PLANET. If you could slice through it you would see that it is made of layers, but only the top layer is made of cold, solid rock. Our home may seem stable, but actually it is continually changing. Some of those changes take millions and millions of years, but others are sudden and can be deadly to life.

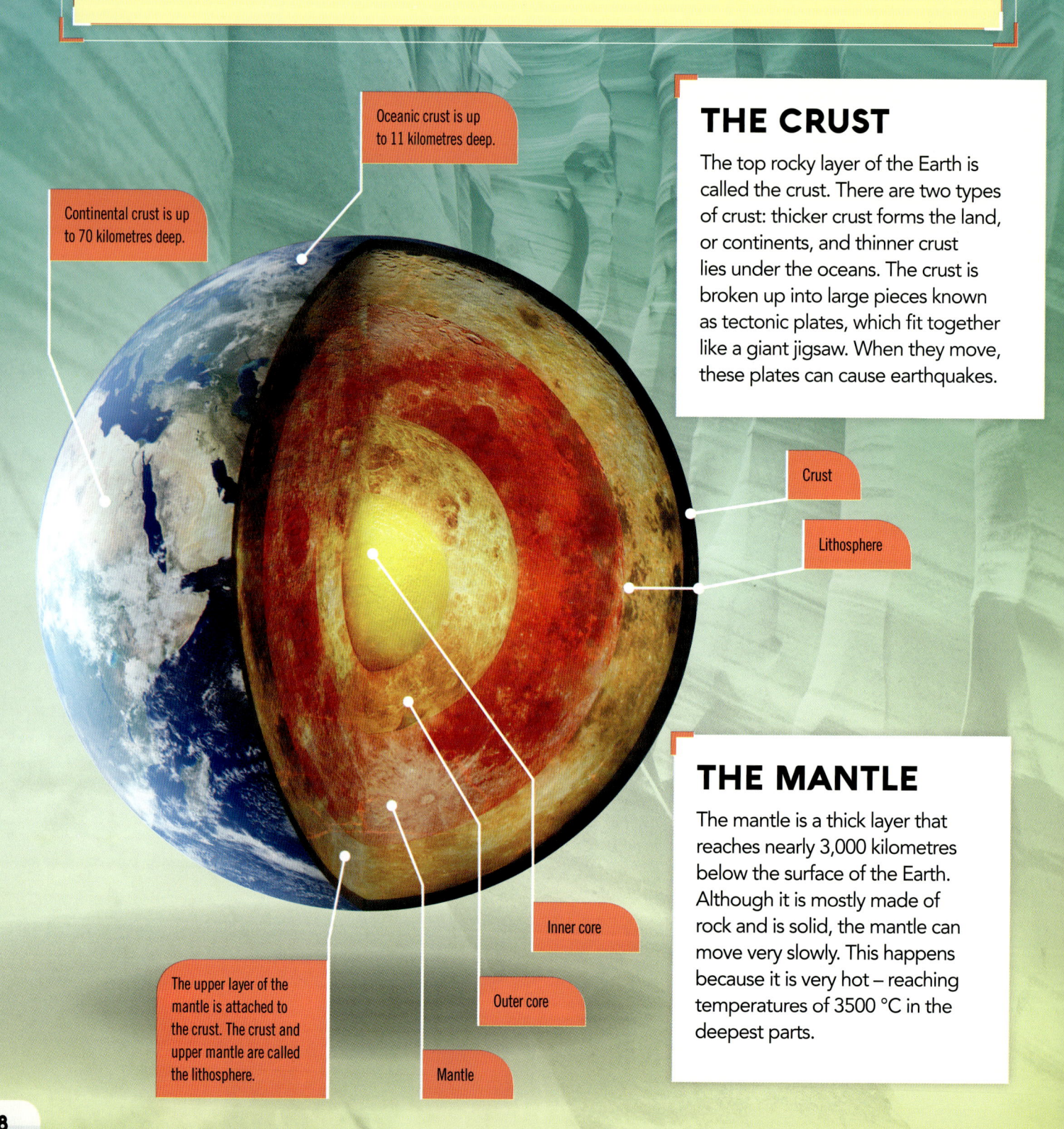

Oceanic crust is up to 11 kilometres deep.

Continental crust is up to 70 kilometres deep.

THE CRUST

The top rocky layer of the Earth is called the crust. There are two types of crust: thicker crust forms the land, or continents, and thinner crust lies under the oceans. The crust is broken up into large pieces known as tectonic plates, which fit together like a giant jigsaw. When they move, these plates can cause earthquakes.

Crust

Lithosphere

Inner core

Outer core

The upper layer of the mantle is attached to the crust. The crust and upper mantle are called the lithosphere.

Mantle

THE MANTLE

The mantle is a thick layer that reaches nearly 3,000 kilometres below the surface of the Earth. Although it is mostly made of rock and is solid, the mantle can move very slowly. This happens because it is very hot – reaching temperatures of 3500 °C in the deepest parts.

THE CORE

The core is the Earth's centre and it is made of the metals nickel and iron. You would have to travel about 6,370 kilometres to reach the centre of the Earth. The core is extremely hot, reaching up to 6,000 °C at its centre. This heat causes the outer layer of the core to turn to liquid, although the metals in the centre are under such pressure they stay in a solid state.

Basalt

ROCKS AND MINERALS

The rocks in the Earth's crust give us the landscapes that we know so well, helping to create tall mountain ranges, deep canyons and vast grassland plains. Rocks all began to form inside the Earth's mantle.

There are three main types of rock:

IGNEOUS ROCKS were once molten (semi-solid) rocks inside the mantle that turned cold and solid when they reached the crust. Lava from volcanoes cools to create igneous rocks such as basalt.

METAMORPHIC ROCKS were once igneous or sedimentary types of rock but have been changed by great temperatures or pressure inside the Earth's crust. Marble, for example, has been changed from a limestone or other similar sedimentary rock.

SEDIMENTARY ROCKS are made from particles of other rocks and minerals that have been broken up and moved by wind, water or ice. They often form in layers. Sandstone is a sedimentary rock that is made of particles of sand.

Marble

Sandstone

ON THE MOVE

EARTH IS AN ACTIVE PLANET. Heat and pressure from deep inside the Earth makes the surface of our planet move all the time. Enormous slabs of crust creep across the planet, creating new oceans, destroying old continents and building mountains. These massive movements happen because of a process called plate tectonics.

HEATING AND COOLING

The heat in the Earth's mantle and crust rises towards the surface of the planet. As these currents of heat move through the Earth they force the rocks in the mantle and crust upwards. At the surface, the rocks cool. They begin to move more slowly and sink down, dragging the tectonic plates with them like a conveyor belt.

SPLITTING AND SEPARATING

Where currents of heat come to the Earth's surface the plates are stretched and pulled apart. This is called a divergent boundary. New rock, called magma, moves up from the mantle. It soon cools and forms new solid rock at the crust. This is how oceans grow and continents are pushed further apart.

Deep underwater, burning magma reaches the surface of the ocean crust and is cooled.

This world map shows all the tectonic plates and where they meet.

North American Plate · Eurasian Plate · North American Plate · Caribbean Plate · Cocos Plate · Arabian Plate · Indian Plate · Philippine Plate · Pacific Plate · Pacific Plate · African Plate · Nazca Plate · South American Plate · Australian Plate · Scotia Plate · Antarctic Plate

CRASHING AND SINKING

Oceanic plates are heavier than continental plates, so in places where they meet, the oceanic plate begins to sink. This is called a convergent boundary and it marks the place where oceans are destroyed as their crust gets sucked into the mantle. There is an enormous convergent boundary that runs along the western coast of South America and as the two plates have crashed into each other the giant Andes Mountain chain has been formed.

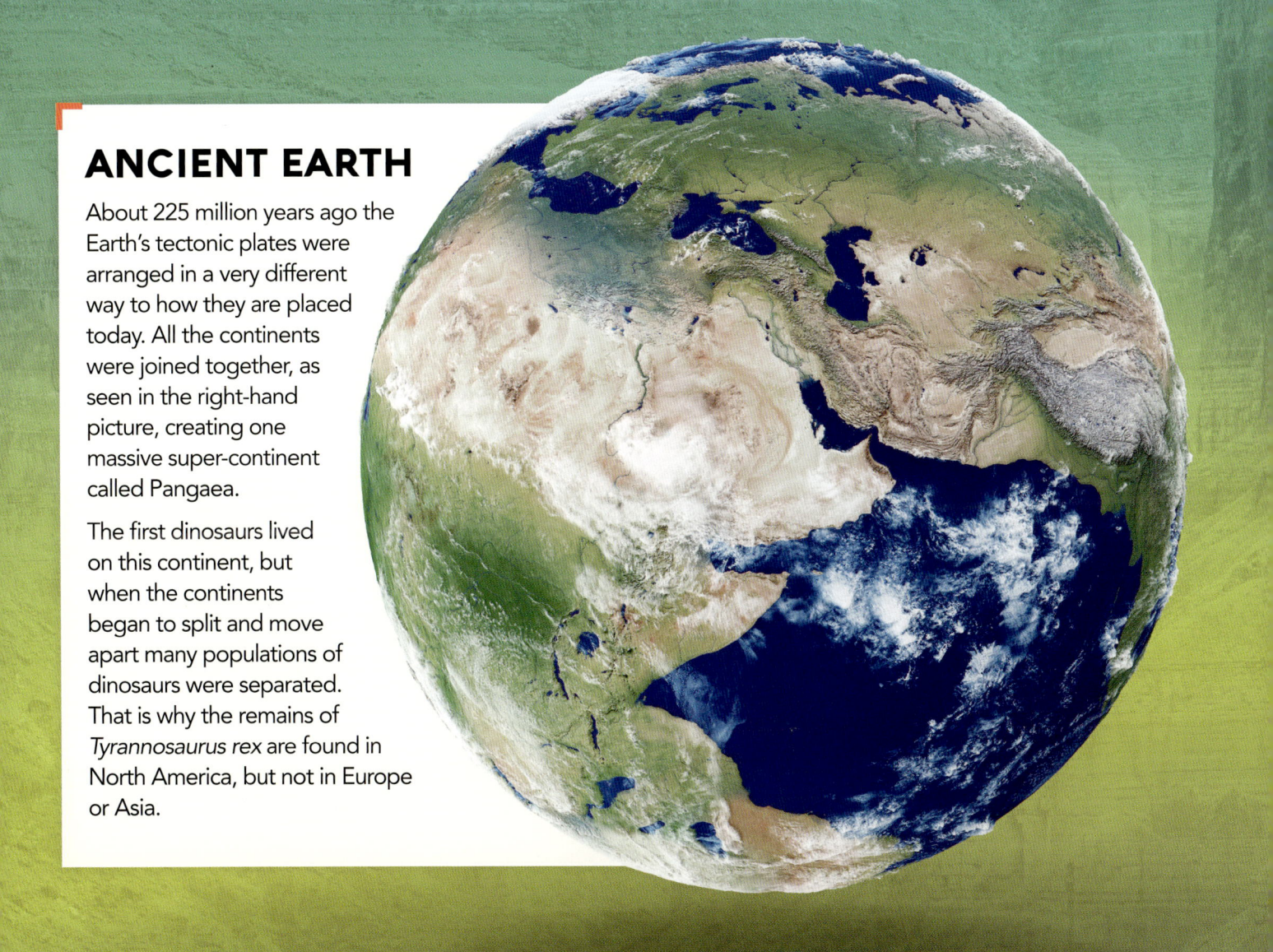

The Andes Mountains make the world's longest mountain chain, at 7,200 kilometres. Water from the Andes flows east, creating the Amazon River, which provides the Amazon Rainforest with an enormous amount of water.

ANCIENT EARTH

About 225 million years ago the Earth's tectonic plates were arranged in a very different way to how they are placed today. All the continents were joined together, as seen in the right-hand picture, creating one massive super-continent called Pangaea.

The first dinosaurs lived on this continent, but when the continents began to split and move apart many populations of dinosaurs were separated. That is why the remains of *Tyrannosaurus rex* are found in North America, but not in Europe or Asia.

FIRE AND FURY

THE FORCES THAT PUSH AND PULL THE EARTH'S CRUST ARE IMMENSE – sometimes too much for even solid rock to bear. When the heat and pressure build they can reach a point when enormous amounts of energy are released, often with catastrophic results.

- Eruption column
- Acid rain
- Crater vent
- Ash fall
- Pyroclastic flow (hot gas and ash)
- Lava flow
- Side vent
- Fumaroles (steam and gases)
- Branch pipe
- Ash and lava layers
- Magma
- Crack
- New land forms
- Ground water

MAGMA AND LAVA

Chambers of magma collect near the Earth's surface, continually fuelled by the heat below, and as more magma moves into them the pressure increases. Eventually, the energy is released as the magma spurts upwards and out of weaker areas in the rocks, flowing as lava. As the lava cools it turns into solid rock and builds up to create a volcano.

ASH AND GASES

When a volcano erupts it is not just lava that covers the surrounding land. Toxic gases may also erupt from the vent, bringing death and devastation to living things nearby. Huge plumes of ash soar into the sky, and can be blown far away by the wind. Over time, the ash and lava become part of the soil and can make surrounding areas more fertile so crops can be grown there.

SHATTERED EARTH

When the Earth's tectonic plates meet and move they can buckle, bend and slip. These movements can release large amounts of energy that cause the land to shake. We call these earthquakes. In towns and cities this can have a devastating impact, as buildings collapse.

Earthquakes in the ocean can set off huge movements of seawater called tsunamis. When a tsunami hits land it can cause flooding and great loss of life.

Buildings were destroyed after two major earthquakes hit Nepal in 2015.

13

DYNAMIC EARTH

HUMAN LIVES ARE TOO SHORT TO WITNESS THE WAY THE WORLD'S BEAUTIFUL LANDSCAPES ARE CHANGED OVER TIME – but the results are all around for us to see and enjoy. Rivers wend their way across continents and mountains rise up from the ground, altering the weather and creating a range of habitats where plants and animals live.

RIVERS

Mountain peaks are cold places, so snow and ice often cap their peaks. In spring the frozen water melts and, together with rainfall, creates streams that flow down to lower ground. The streams join up to create larger rivers that flow to the sea. These rivers help spread minerals from mountain rocks into the soil, and they provide fresh water for plants, animals and humans.

MOUNTAIN BUILDING

The tectonic plate that bears the country of India has moved 2,000 kilometres northwards in 50 million years. As it moved, the sea between the Indian plate and the Asian plate was swallowed up entirely and the rocks beneath were crumpled into the mighty Himalayan mountains.

Where once there were fish and octopuses, now there are long-haired yaks and spotted snow leopards in the Himalayas.

The Needles are tall white peaks that stand in the sea on England's south coast. They are made of chalk and have been eroded by waves to create their peculiar shapes.

EROSION

As water flows it wears away at the surrounding ground, this is called erosion. As a river erodes its way through rock it creates valleys, waterfalls or canyons. The Grand Canyon in North America has been created by the Colorado River. Over the course of 17 million years the Colorado has carved a canyon that is 446 kilometres long and up to 1.6 kilometres deep, reaching layers of rock that are 2.5 billion years old!

WAVES AND WIND

River water is not the only eroding power in the landscape. Waves and wind can also batter rocks and soil, carving cliffs and creating strange landforms such as columns of rock, arches, caves and rock stacks.

GLACIERS

A glacier is a solid river of ice that forms in cold places, especially in polar regions and high mountains. The ice moves slowly, creeping down to lower-lying ground. As they move, glaciers break the rock and carry it with them. The pieces of broken rock scour the ground below, further eroding it to create a U-shaped valley.

The Jakobshavn Glacier is one of the fastest in the world, moving at up to 20 metres a day. It is also melting faster than it is growing, possibly as a result of global climate change.

WATER

THERE ARE MANY REASONS WHY EARTH IS ABLE TO SUPPORT LIFE, but one of the most important is that our home is a wet world. Water is essential for life, and all of the first organisms lived in the salty water of the oceans and seas until about 440 million years ago.

Condensation

Evaporation

WHAT IS WATER?

Each molecule, or tiny particle, of water is made from one atom of oxygen and two atoms of hydrogen. Water exists elsewhere in the Universe, but on Earth we have the perfect range of temperatures for it to exist as a solid, liquid and gas. When liquid water is cooled it becomes ice and when it is heated it becomes water vapour.

About 97 per cent of the world's water is salty and it is found in oceans, seas and some lakes. The rest of the water is fresh and exists in the atmosphere, glaciers, rivers, lakes and the ground.

WHERE DOES WATER COME FROM?

No one knows how the first water appeared on Earth, but it may have come from an asteroid that smashed into the planet, or from magma that erupted onto the Earth's surface as water vapour and cooled to become rain. Eventually enough rain fell to fill the oceans. The water in the oceans and seas is salty, but rainwater and the water that flows in rivers is fresh water, without salt.

Animals and plants need fresh water to survive, though some can go a long time without it.

Precipitation

Precipitation

Snow melt

Surface flow

Evaporation

Plant uptake

Groundwater flow

THE WATER CYCLE

Today's water moves around the world in the seas and in the rivers, and in the air as clouds. There is also water beneath our feet, trapped in rocks or in the soil. This is called groundwater. This way that water moves around the world is called the water cycle.

When water in the oceans and on land warms up it evaporates – turns into water vapour – and rises into the sky where it forms clouds. When it cools again it falls as rain. Rainwater flows underground to become groundwater, or it flows through rivers and returns to the oceans. When water evaporates it leaves the salt behind, which is why the oceans are salty, but rainfall and rivers are not.

THE WORLD OCEAN

THE WORLD'S OCEANS AND SEAS COVER TWO-THIRDS OF THE EARTH'S SURFACE WITH 1.4 MILLION CUBIC KILOMETRES OF WATER. Although we divide the planet's salty water into five oceans and about 20 seas, they are actually connected together in one giant body of water we call the World Ocean.

OCEAN DATA

The five oceans in order of size are: the Pacific, the Atlantic, the Indian, the Southern and the Arctic. The average depth of the World Ocean is 3,800 metres and although its average temperature is about 17 °C, scientists have discovered that the top layer of the ocean has increased in temperature in the last 100 years. The World Ocean represents an enormous home to billions of animals and plants, making it the largest habitat on the planet.

LIGHT AND SHADE

Sunlight passes through the top layer of the ocean water, which means that plants and seaweed can live there. Deeper down, more sunlight is absorbed until, at around 1,000 metres deep, there is no sunlight and the ocean turns inky black. Although the deep ocean is dark, there are many strange animals that manage to survive. Some of them even produce their own light to find prey and mates.

The angler fish uses the light on its head to attract prey close to its jaws.

DEEP SEA MYSTERY

More people have walked on the Moon than have explored the deepest parts of the ocean, making this environment one of the most mysterious on the planet. The Mariana Trench in the Pacific is the lowest point of the World Ocean, almost 11 kilometres from the water surface. The enormous pressure of water in the deep ocean makes this a very dangerous place for humans, but in 2019 a deep-sea submersible called *Limiting Factor* visited the sea bed and found species of sea creatures never seen before… as well as a plastic bag and food wrappers.

Explorer Victor Vescovo descended 10,927 metres to the seafloor – deeper than any human has travelled before.

SUPER SEA

The Pacific Ocean is bigger than all of the world's land put together, but it is surrounded by divergent boundaries so it shrinks by about 500 square kilometres a year. Humans take vast quantities of fish from the Pacific, which supplies about 60 per cent of all fish that humans catch from the World Ocean. We also take valuable minerals and fuels, such as oil and gas, from the seabed where they formed millions of years ago.

Oil tankers carry oil across the oceans but occasionally they accidentally release this black fuel into the sea. It can cause widespread pollution, killing marine life and birds.

ACTIVE OCEANS

WATER FLOWS THROUGH ALL THE OCEANS, CARRYING LIVING ORGANISMS AROUND THE PLANET. Large movements of water flowing through the oceans are called currents and they play an extremely important role in keeping the planet healthy and full of life.

SUN AND SEA

The Earth is warmest around the Equator – an imaginary line that runs around the centre of the planet, dividing it into two halves or hemispheres. Areas just above and below the Equator are closer to the Sun all year round and receive around 12 hours of sunlight every day of the year.

The tropical oceans are particularly warm. The polar oceans, however, are further from the Sun and experience long winters when the days are short and the weather turns cold enough to freeze the surface water.

THE GLOBAL CONVEYOR

The difference in temperatures around the World Ocean creates vast currents of water. As water warms it rises to the surface and flows away from the tropics. As it reaches the cooler poles the water loses its heat and sinks down to the seabed. This giant movement of water is called the Global Conveyor and it carries over 100 times the amount of water than the Amazon River.

The Global Conveyor distributes water, food and other nutrients around the world and helps to balance the temperature of the planet.

Warm surface flow
Cool subsurface flow

WAVES

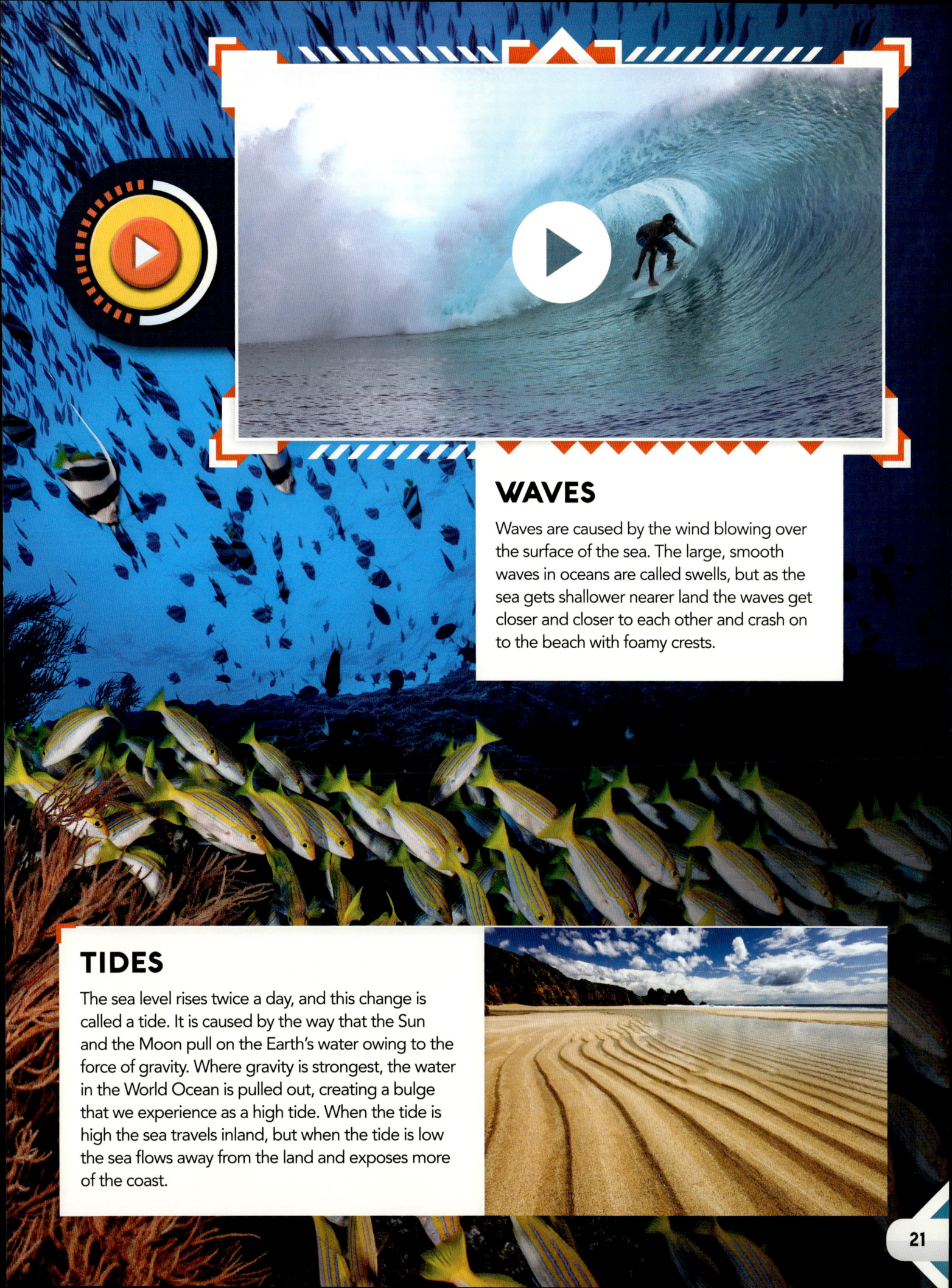

Waves are caused by the wind blowing over the surface of the sea. The large, smooth waves in oceans are called swells, but as the sea gets shallower nearer land the waves get closer and closer to each other and crash on to the beach with foamy crests.

TIDES

The sea level rises twice a day, and this change is called a tide. It is caused by the way that the Sun and the Moon pull on the Earth's water owing to the force of gravity. Where gravity is strongest, the water in the World Ocean is pulled out, creating a bulge that we experience as a high tide. When the tide is high the sea travels inland, but when the tide is low the sea flows away from the land and exposes more of the coast.

THE ATMOSPHERE

A THICK BLANKET OF GASES SURROUNDS EARTH. This is called the atmosphere and without it life would be impossible. The atmosphere contains gases that plants and animals need to survive, but it also protects us from the Sun's deadliest rays and it creates our weather and climates.

EXOSPHERE
700–190,000 KM

THERMOSPHERE
80–700 KM

MESOSPHERE
50–80 KM

STRATOSPHERE
12–50 KM

TROPOSPHERE
0–12 KM

FIRST AIR

The first atmosphere on Earth was made of helium and hydrogen gases. Then gases, such as nitrogen, carbon dioxide and water vapour escaped from volcanoes and the atmosphere changed. By around 2.7 billion years ago there were tiny organisms in the oceans that used carbon dioxide to make food. During this process they made oxygen, which was released into the atmosphere. Oxygen is the gas that we breathe.

LAYERS AND GASES

The atmosphere forms layers around the Earth. The bottom layer is called the troposphere and this is where living things are found and where the weather exists. It is about 16 kilometres thick at the equator and 8 kilometres thick over the North and South Pole. The air in the atmosphere is mostly nitrogen and oxygen.

WATER IN THE AIR

When water evaporates it turns into a gas and floats in the air. The amount of water held in the air is known as the relative humidity and warm air can hold more water than cool air, so the humidity is usually higher in tropical areas than in the polar regions.

Ferns are plants that thrive in humid forests. The air is damp enough for water-loving mosses to grow on tree trunks.

SOLIDS IN AIR

The atmosphere also contains billions upon billions of tiny particles of solids such as smoke, ash, pollution, particles from volcanic eruptions, pollen from plants and even tiny particles of sand from desert storms. Warm currents of air keep these particles airborne and can move them great distances.

THE GREENHOUSE EFFECT

The Sun's great energy heats up the air, bathing the Earth in warmth and helping things to live and grow. The atmosphere helps keep much of that energy close to the Earth. This is called the greenhouse effect, and the gases in the atmosphere that cause it are called greenhouse gases.

Without an atmosphere, the planet would be too cold for life. However, in the last few hundred years humans have added more greenhouses gases, such as carbon dioxide, to the atmosphere. This has trapped the heat, warming up the planet.

CLIMATE AND WEATHER

THE EARTH'S ATMOSPHERE CONTROLS WEATHER AND CLIMATE. This has an important effect on where animals and plants live. The most extreme weathers and climates can be very challenging, and in some instances they are deadly.

WHAT'S THE DIFFERENCE?

The weather is the rain, sunshine, humidity and wind that are in one place at one time. Weather can change quickly but it can also vary between different seasons. The climate is the pattern of weather that is normal in a place over a longer period of time.

CONTROLLING THE WEATHER

The weather depends on many things that can change quickly, which is one reason why it can be very hard to predict! The length of the day, the season, the amount of water in the air, air pressure, the strength of the sunshine and the movement of warm air in currents around the atmosphere are all important factors for creating weather. Even the landscape affects the weather, with rain clouds often forming alongside mountain slopes.

BIOMES

The type of climate in an area affects what plants can grow, and which animals can thrive there. A place's climate and its animals and plants are called a biome. Deserts, tropical rainforests, mountains and grasslands are all examples of biomes.

The fynbos of South Africa is a unique biome that experiences hot, dry summers and cool, wet winters. It is home to more than 9,000 species of plant, many of which grow nowhere else on Earth.

SEASONS

The position of the Earth as it orbits the Sun, and the way that the planet is tilted on its axis, gives many parts of the world four main seasons: spring, summer, autumn and winter. In tropical regions the climate remains similar throughout the year, but they can experience dry and wet seasons instead.

FROM POLES TO TROPICS

Although weather can vary from day to day, there are weather patterns that create regions with similar climates. There are many climate regions but they are divided into three main bands: polar, temperate and tropical.

The polar regions have least sunlight and warmth and the climate is cold with little or no rain.

Temperate regions lie between the poles and the tropics, and they usually experience mild weather with warm summers and cool winters.

Tropical regions are the hottest and sunniest places throughout the year.

25

EXTREME WEATHER

FROM MASSIVE MONSOON FLOODS TO TERRIFYING TWISTERS, THE WEATHER CAN BE DEADLY, UNPREDICTABLE AND WILD. These natural forces can wreak havoc on our Earth, damaging habitats and destroying lives.

HURRICANES AND TWISTERS

Hurricane winds are vast spirals of warm and wet air that develop over the oceans and move inland. A hurricane, which is also known as a typhoon or a cyclone, can spin at speeds of more than 200 kilometres an hour, bringing rain and floods as well as ripping up trees and buildings. A twister, or tornado, is a smaller, faster, spiral of wind. Twisters normally spin for a short time, but they are powerful enough to destroy homes and forests.

MONSOON WIND AND WATER

As the hot Sun warms the Indian Ocean, the wind picks up lots of water vapour and moves onto the land. This is the monsoon wind and it brings heavy rainfall to parts of Asia from June to September. The rain can cause flooding, especially in areas where plants and trees have been stripped away to create fields for crops and animals.

This aerial photo of farmland in Malawi shows monsoon flooding.

SANDSTORMS AND WILDFIRES

When the weather turns dry for a long time, animals and plants may struggle to survive. This is called a drought, but long periods of dry weather can have other consequences too, such as sandstorms and wildfires. Winds can pick up particles of sand in a desert and carry them great distances, creating sandstorms that can travel at speeds of 90 kilometres an hour. When plants dry out they can catch fire easily and cause entire forests to burn in wildfires.

THUNDER AND LIGHTNING

Thunderstorms form where warm, wet air crashes into patches of cold air, and wind makes the warm air rise up through the sky and spin. As the warm air rises it builds into storm clouds. It begins to lose energy and cools down, and the water vapour turns to rain. A build up of electricity in the storm cloud can cause giant lightning flashes to rip through the sky. Thunder is the sound that the lightning makes.

SNOW AND ICE

When water vapour freezes in the air it exists as tiny ice crystals; when these crystals clump together they form snowflakes. It may be light, fluffy and beautiful, but snow can fall in dangerous blizzards that are whipped through the air by strong winds. When snow piles up on mountains it can become unstable, and sudden snowfalls, called avalanches, can bury homes.

Avalanches can be triggered by the weather, but also by skiers, snowmobiles and hikers.

2 WONDER OF LIFE

THE SMALLEST LIVING THINGS ON EARTH ARE FAR TOO SMALL TO SEE WITH THE NAKED EYE. The biggest living things include enormous trees that grow towards the sky and blue whales that swim through the oceans, eating shrimp-like animals no bigger than your finger! Since life first began on Earth, an enormous variety of organisms have lived and died. Today there are at least 1.5 million different species of animal, 140,000 species of fungi and 380,000 species of plant.

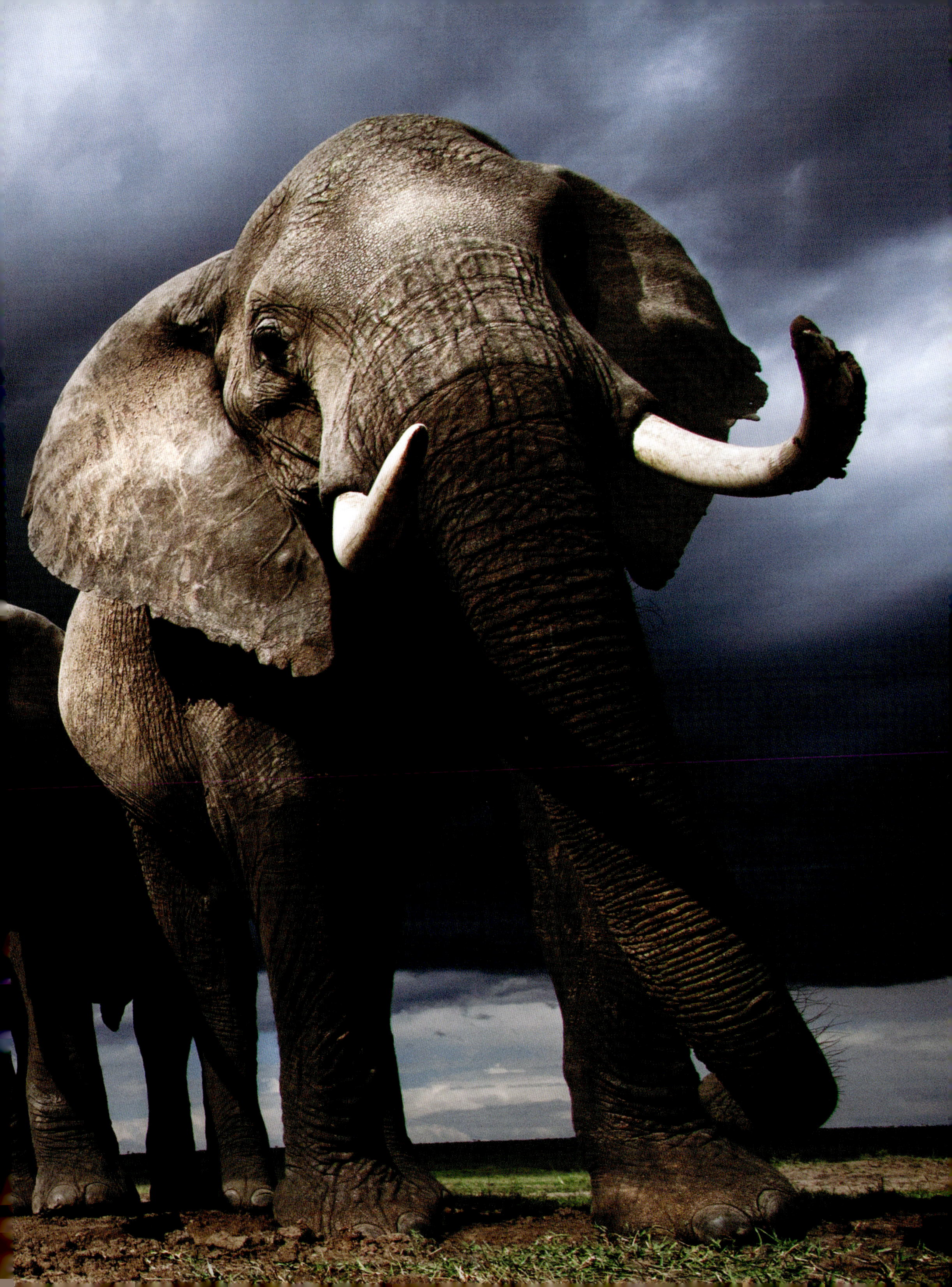

LIFE BEGINS

WE HAVE LEARNED MUCH ABOUT OUR PLANET, BUT THE STORY OF EARTH STILL HOLDS ONE GREAT MYSTERY. Unlike anywhere else in the known Universe there is life here – lots of it – but we still do not know how, or when it all began. Scientists believe life on Earth began in water, possibly in shallow pools that were rich in chemicals, or deep in the ocean where chemicals poured out from the crust.

TIMELINE OF LIFE

The Earth's history is divided into chunks of time that help scientists identify how life developed and changed.

Archaen Era
4 to 2.5 billion years ago
Life began in the Archaen Era but it remained quite simple for about 1.5 billion years.

Proterozoic Era
2.5 billion to 541 million years ago
Living things began to use sunlight for energy and the first animals evolved.

Palaeozoic Era
541 to 252 million years ago
There was an explosion of life and a huge number of different animals and plants developed and moved onto land.

Mesozoic Era
252 to 66 million years ago
Dinosaurs ruled the planet, and small mammals also thrived until a meteorite crashed into Earth and dinosaurs were wiped out.

Cenozoic Era
66 million years ago to present day
Mammals took over from reptiles and, in the form of humans, have eventually come to dominate and change the planet.

FIRST SIGNS

There were living things on Earth at least 3.8 billion years ago, but life may have begun before then, when the world was still very hot and active with volcanoes. Chemicals began to react together to form molecules that eventually became enclosed in cells.

A cell is the basic building block of living things. Early cells got their energy from chemicals in water, but eventually they were able to get their energy from sunlight.

IT BEGAN WITH BACTERIA

One of the reasons it is difficult to know how life began is that there is little evidence of early life on Earth. Scientists rely on fossils to discover more about early life, and some of the most important fossils are of tiny organisms called stromatolites. They are a type of bacteria that grew in mounds 3.4 billion years ago – and still exist today.

WHAT IS A FOSSIL?

A fossil is the remains of a long-dead animal or plant that has turned to stone, such as the ammonites shown here. When most organisms die they rot away, but occasionally their remains are turned to stone by minerals. This is called fossilisation and it is most successful with hard body parts such as bones, teeth, claws and shells. People who study animals and plants that lived long ago are called palaeontologists, and their study of early life has revealed many secrets about Earth's past.

CHANGING CLIMATES

The Earth has gone through many periods of time when the climates have been very different to the ones we experience today. Periods of ice and snow covering large parts of the land, and times when the planet has warmed up so much that there was no ice at the poles, and the sea level was higher than it is today. When the climate changes the animals and plants that live on Earth must adapt to the new conditions, or die.

PREHISTORIC LIFE

LONG AGO THE WORLD WAS HOME TO POWERFUL DINOSAURS, enormous dragonflies that were the size of birds and flying reptiles with large, leathery wings. During the history of life on Earth there have been countless battles for survival that have seen animals and plants develop to cope with an ever-changing environment – and many of those organisms looked different to the ones we have today.

PREHISTORIC PLANTS

The first plants were tiny and lived in the sea. By 440 million years ago there were plants on land too, but they were simple and small. By 300 million years ago the land was covered in large, green fern-trees, horsetails and mosses. Many of these were buried in swamps and eventually fossilized into the hard black rock we know as coal.

Coal is a type of fossil fuel, which means that it releases greenhouse gases when it is burned. This contributes to the modern problem of global climate change.

MARINE MONSTERS

Today's scorpions are mostly small enough to fit in the palm of your hand and they live in hot, dry environments. But 400 million years ago giant scorpions lived in the sea – called Eurypterids, these sea scorpions could reach an impressive 2.5 metres long!

Ammonites (see p30–31) were shelled sea creatures that survived for more than 300 million years before being wiped out at the same time as the dinosaurs. The largest ammonites weighed as much as a car. They are related to modern octopuses.

Sea scorpions may have used their spiked tails to slash their prey.

FLYING ANIMALS

There was more oxygen in the atmosphere in the past, and this meant that insects could grow bigger than today. Giant dragonflies swooped through the air to feast on smaller bugs. Some of them had wingspans of more than 70 centimetres! During the Age of the Dinosaurs there were large flying reptiles called pterosaurs, and the first birds appeared around 150 million years ago.

AGE OF THE DINOSAURS

Dinosaurs ruled the planet for about 150 million years. The largest were the giant sauropods that used their long necks to reach high into trees to eat leaves. Tyrannosaurs and other carnivores had powerful limbs, long claws and enormous teeth for catching and killing other beasts to eat. Today's palaeontologists are uncovering the fossilised remains of many new species of dinosaur. They use them to work out how these incredible animals lived, and why they died out 66 million years ago.

MEGAFAUNA OF THE ICE AGE

Megafauna, or large animals, thrived during the Ice Ages when the world's climate cooled right down and ice covered the land and seas. There were long-tusked mammoths with thick, shaggy fur, large woolly rhinos and sabre-toothed cats. One of these predators, known as *Smilodon*, had teeth that grew up to 30 centimetres long!

Triceratops probably used it its three horns and huge neck frill to defend itself from dinosaurs such as *Tyrannosaurus rex*.

EVOLUTION AND EXTINCTION

THE WAY THAT ANIMALS AND PLANTS HAVE CHANGED AND DEVELOPED OVER TIME IS CALLED EVOLUTION. It is an incredible process that allows living things to adapt to suit the world around them. When an organism cannot adapt well enough to survive, its species dies out forever. This is extinction.

THE CODE OF LIFE

The cells of living things contain molecules called deoxyribonucleic acid, or DNA for short. It contains all the codes necessary to instruct cells to grow, reproduce and function. DNA contains sections called genes, and these are passed from one generation to the next. For example, in a bird some genes may contain the codes for feather colour and others may contain the codes for size and shape of beak.

NATURAL SELECTION

Animals that are best-suited to their environment are more likely to survive long enough to reproduce, or have young, than others. That means their genes, and the characteristics that helped them to survive, are passed onto the next generation. This is called natural selection. A giraffe with a long neck, for example, can reach leaves that shorter-necked giraffes cannot reach. A well-fed giraffe is more likely to reproduce, and if its young inherit its longer neck they are more likely to survive too.

ARTIFICIAL SELECTION

For thousands of years humans have been using evolution to breed better crops and livestock that are more useful to us. This is called artificial selection. All domestic dogs, for example, have been bred from the grey wolf to develop characteristics that we favour. In the past, we bred dogs that were good at protecting our homes and livestock, but today we usually breed dogs for their looks and friendly personalities.

Birds began their history as flying feathered dinosaurs, and they also survived the mass extinction event.

NATURAL EXTINCTION

Extinctions are a normal part of evolution because they allow organisms to improve their ability to survive. Dinosaurs went extinct 66 million years ago after a giant asteroid crashed into Earth and damaged the worldwide environment with fire, toxic gases and a drop in global temperature. This triggered one of a number of mass extinctions that have taken place. However, small mammals that lived alongside the dinosaurs were able to cope with the changed world, and eventually evolved into the huge range of mammals that live today – including humans.

MODERN EXTINCTIONS

Scientists believe the world is going through another mass extinction event today, but this one is caused by human activity. The natural environment is facing a huge challenge as we pollute the air and water, destroy habitats and hunt animals to extinction.

Many species of frog and toad are at great risk of extinction. They have lost their natural habitats and suffer from a disease that may have been caused by the changing climate.

35

KINGDOMS OF LIFE

ORGANISMS ON OUR LIVING PLANET ARE DIVIDED INTO MAJOR GROUPS, OR KINGDOMS, which help us understand how they are all related to each other and how they evolved. The science of sorting organisms into different groups is called classification.

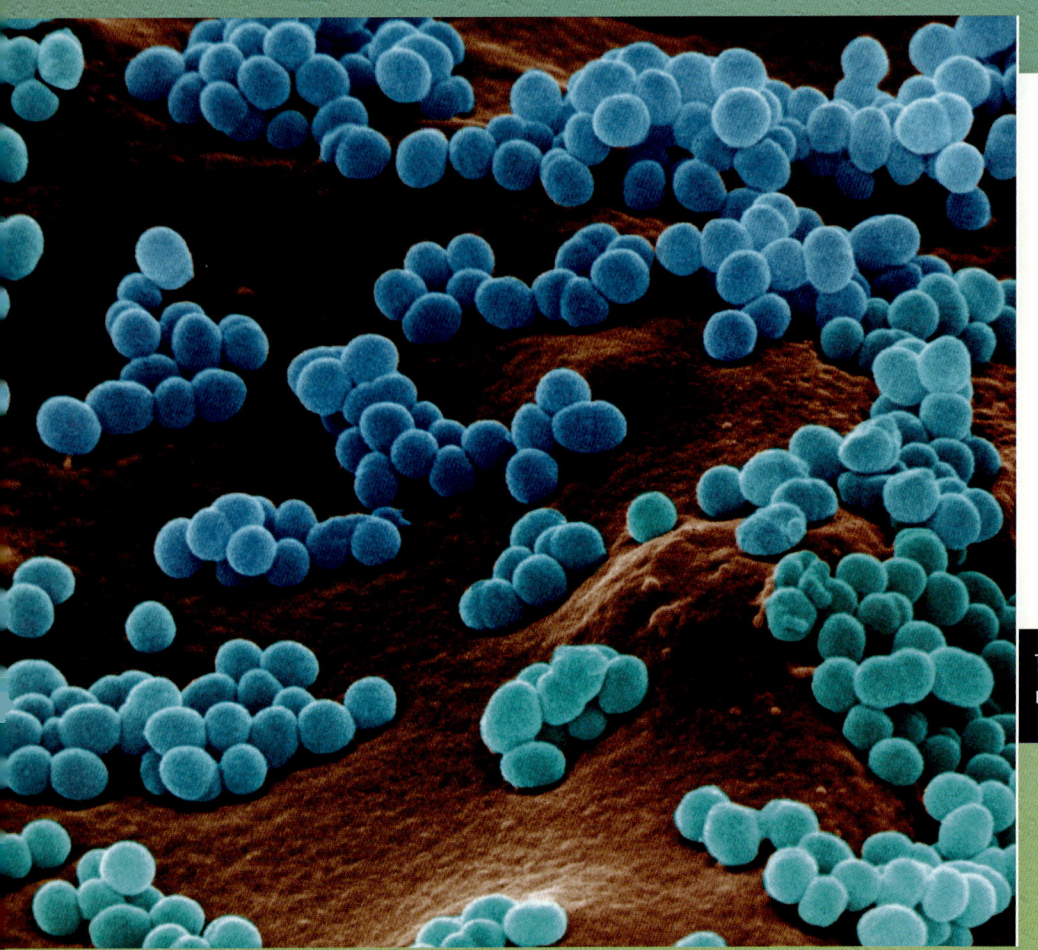

BACTERIA

The smallest living things are bacteria and they cannot be seen without the aid of a microscope. Bacteria are simple organisms. They survive in every habitat on Earth and were amongst the first things to live. The kingdom of bacteria contains more living things than all the other kingdoms put together.

This image of *Micrococcus* bacteria has been magnified, so it is 21,000 times its size.

PROTISTS

Microscopic animals and plants are classified in a kingdom called Protista. Most protists are made up of just one cell but they are more complex than bacteria. They usually live in water and many of them photosynthesise.

Living things that are too small to be seen with the naked eye are known as microorganisms. They include bacteria, protists and many fungi.

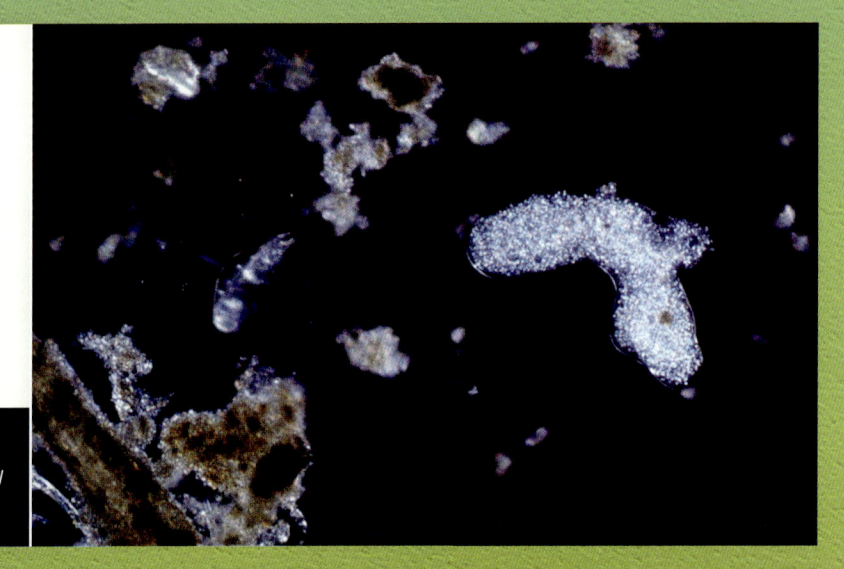

FUNGI

Fungi is a group of living organisms that include mushrooms and toadstools as well as much smaller forms of life such as moulds. Fungi are often mistaken for plants, but they are more closely related to animals, and they digest their food rather than photosynthesise.

Fungi are some of nature's recyclers. Many types grow and feed on dead plants and animals.

PLANTS

Plants need light to live, grow and make their food. They use a green pigment to capture sunlight, which is why most plants are green. Algae are plants that live in the oceans and seas. Through the history of evolution many plants have come to rely on animals to survive, especially to help them make and spread their seeds.

Green algae are plants that live in water.

ANIMALS

Unlike plants, animals need to eat food. These are the most varied organisms on Earth and animals have been so successful in the fight for life that they have adapted to survive in habitats from the deep sea to the tops of mountains. While many animals have simple bodies, others have evolved highly complex body parts, behaviours and lifestyles.

Fennec foxes live in dry places where food is scarce. They use their huge ears to listen for bugs.

PLANT LIFE

A PLANT IS A LIVING ORGANISM THAT IS MADE UP OF MANY CELLS AND USES SUNLIGHT TO MAKE ITS OWN FOOD. Most plants grow from seeds. Duckweeds are the smallest plants, at just 1 millimetre long. The tallest plants are coast redwood trees that grow more than 100 metres high. Each redwood tree can have as many as 550 million leaves!

SIMPLE PLANTS

The earliest plants to evolve were ones that grew from tiny spores, not seeds, and their relatives are still alive today. Mosses, liverworts, ferns and horsetails all belong to this group of seedless plants. They often prefer to grow in damp habitats, and are mostly small.

CONIFERS

Coniferous plants grow their seeds in cones, not flowers. Many conifers, such as pine, fir and spruce, are trees and most of them keep their leaves all year so they are sometimes known as 'evergreens'. Conifers are good at surviving in places with harsh, cold winters and many of them can cope with long periods of dry weather.

The thick bark of a conifer helps to protect the inside of the tree from extreme heat and cold.

FLOWERING PLANTS

Most plants belong to a group called angiosperms, which are plants that grow flowers that produce seeds. Flowering plants evolved around 135 million years ago and they are now found all over the world, from deserts and mountains, to ponds and rainforests.

Seaweeds are green, brown or red. They usually live at the coast and can cope with powerful winds, waves and tidal flows of water.

ALGAE

Most types of algae are tiny – just one cell big – and are often classified in the group of microorganisms known as protists. These single-celled organisms often join together in vast groups called colonies that turn water green. Algae flourished in oceans, rivers and lakes long before plants evolved on land and they still live in water today. Algae that have many cells are called seaweed.

CYCLE OF LIFE

When plants die they rot away into the soil or water, and are slowly decomposed by the small animals and fungi that feed on them. This fertilises the soil, so other plants can grow there. When living things rot they give off greenhouse gases that can be damaging to the atmosphere, but these gases can be used as a fuel to cook, generate electricity and heat water, especially in places where people do not have access to other types of fuel.

HOW PLANTS LIVE

PLANTS ARE LIVING THINGS, WHICH MEANS THEY NEED TO BE ABLE TO BREATHE, reproduce, sense the world around them and use food to grow and change. Over the millions of years since they evolved, plants have adapted to find homes in all sorts of habitats, and have found many different ways to live successfully.

BASIC STRUCTURE

Most plants grow in soil. They use roots to anchor themselves in the ground and take up water and nutrients. Stems grow above the ground, and leaves spread out to absorb sunlight. Water moves through the stem in tubes called xylem vessels and food made in the leaves is goes to other parts of the plant through phloem tubes.

PHOTOSYNTHESIS

The word 'photosynthesis' means 'making with light'. Plants use the energy in sunlight to turn carbon dioxide and water into sugary food. Photosynthesis takes place in the leaves where a green pigment, called chlorophyll, captures sunlight. Leaves lose their chlorophyll when they die, which is why leaves turn red, brown or yellow as they age.

BREATHING

Plants take in carbon dioxide gas and release water vapour and oxygen gas as waste products of photosynthesis. Gases pass in and out of plants through tiny holes on their leaves, called stomata. The oxygen that plants make is the gas that animals need to breathe.

MEAT-EATERS

Some plants live in shady places where the soil has few nutrients. Photosynthesis does not produce enough food in these conditions, so they have evolved as meat-eaters. Venus flytraps, sundew plants and pitcher plants trap bugs which are dissolved and absorbed by the plant.

Sundew plants grow sweet, sticky droplets on stalks. Bugs land on them, but cannot escape.

USEFUL PLANTS

Plants are an essential source of food for many animals, including humans. They are also used to make homes, from nests to houses. People use trees to make wood, paper and cardboard, and in many parts of the world wood is still an important fuel for light, heat and cooking.

A harvest mouse uses its sharp teeth to cut blades of grass and make them into a cosy home.

FLOWERS AND SEEDS

MOST PLANTS USE FLOWERS AND SEEDS TO REPRODUCE AND MANY OF THEM NEED ANIMALS – especially insects – to help them in this important job. That's why many flowers are brightly-coloured and smell good. Flowering plants and insects have evolved at the same time, and they share a close and essential relationship that we all rely on to survive.

FLOWERS

Colourful petals and perfume attract bugs to the centre of the flower. It contains a plant's organs of reproduction, including male and female parts. The male parts are called stamens and they produce a yellow dust called pollen. The female parts include an ovary, which makes eggs that will become seeds once they have been fertilised.

Flowers make nectar to attract insects that will pollinate them.

Bees visit flowers to collect pollen and nectar, a sugary liquid that they use to make honey for their grubs to feed on.

FERTILISATION

Bugs, mammals and birds are all able to help fertilise a plant by transferring the pollen of one plant to the stigma of another. The pollen grows down to the egg in the plant's ovary and joins with it. This is called fertilisation, and at this point the egg can begin to grow and change. It will grow into a seed and the ovary around it protects it as it grows. Ovaries can grow into fruits or nuts that tempt animals to eat them.

As bees move around a flower they transfer pollen to a female part, called a stigma. This is pollination.

SEED DISPERSAL

Seeds need to leave the plant and find a new place to grow. When animals eat the plant, the seeds can pass through their body and end up on the ground where they grow when the conditions are just right. Some seeds are prickly, and get caught on animals' fur, while others grow in pods that explode open, shooting the seeds away from the parent plant. Many seeds are small and light so the wind can carry them away.

The seeds of a dandelion plant are so light they can float away on a breeze.

When a seed begins to grow into a plant it is germinating.

GERMINATION

Seeds contain food inside them, so as soon as the conditions are right they are ready to burst into life. Most seeds need water, warms and darkness to start to grow. Small white roots grow first and then shoots grow up towards the light. Timelapse videos can show us quickly how a plant can grow.

FUNGI

MUSHROOMS, TOADSTOOLS AND MOULDS ALL BELONG TO A GROUP OF ORGANISMS CALLED FUNGI. They are the third most common living things on Earth after bacteria and protists. About 135,000 species of fungi have been discovered so far.

MICRO TO MEGA

Most fungi are microscopic organisms that are found almost everywhere on Earth, from dry deserts to the surface of human skin. The largest organism ever found, however, is also a fungus. It is a giant honey fungus that lives underground in forests. The largest specimen discovered is believed to cover nearly 10 square kilometres and is possibly more than 8,000 years old!

Some mushrooms are bioluminescent — this means they glow in the dark.

MUSHROOMS AND TOADSTOOLS

Mushrooms and toadstools are the parts of fungi that we can often see growing on rotting plants and trees or in the soil. These are the parts that produce spores, which are similar to seeds. One mushroom or toadstool can release half a million spores in just one minute. The spores are so tiny they are easily carried a long way on the wind.

The paper-thin layers under a mushroom cap are called gills. This is where the spores are made.

USEFUL FUNGI

Fungi decompose, or break down, dead animals and plants so the nutrients they contain can return to the soil. This helps reduce disease and means that habitats become places where new life can start, not vast graveyards of dead organisms. We also eat many fungi, and use them to make bread, cheese and even soy sauce! Scientists have used fungi to develop medicines, such as penicillin, that tackle deadly bacterial infections.

DANGER!

Many types of fungi are poisonous and have bright colours to warn animals to stay away. However, many plain fungi are dangerous to eat too. Smaller types of fungi can infect animals and plants, spreading disease and causing harm.

INVERTEBRATE LIFE

MOST ANIMALS ARE INVERTEBRATES – AT LEAST 97 PER CENT OF SPECIES DON'T HAVE A BACKBONE. They were the first animals to evolve and they are found all over the world. Many invertebrates have soft bodies, but others are protected by tough outer skins or shells.

SIMPLE SPONGES

Some of the simplest animals are sponges and they have been in the seas for at least 570 million years. They have minerals that help to give their bodies strength and support. Sponges don't have legs, hearts or brains and they feed by extracting tiny particles of food from the water.

Tube sponges are attached to the seabed, or coral, and cannot move.

STINGING CNIDARIANS

Cnidarians (pronounced without the 'c') are invertebrates that have a tube-like body and live in water. They have tentacles that are equipped with stinging cells, which they use to kill their prey or defend themselves from attack. Jellyfish, sea anemones and corals are all types of cnidarians.

The mauve stinger jellyfish is covered in stinging cells. Their sting causes pain that can last for a couple of weeks.

WRIGGLY WORMS

Worms have managed to make their homes in a huge range of habitats. Billions of tiny worms live in the soil and in the bodies of other animals, but the largest ones include the impressive bootlace worm, which lives in the sea. It can grow more than 50 metres long!

Blue starfish are common in the shallow seas of the Pacific and Indian Oceans.

Some worms have smooth, simple bodies but others are divided into parts, or segments.

MIGHTY MOLLUSCS

This group of invertebrates includes giant squid and octopuses as well as the humble garden slug and snail. Shelled sea creatures such as mussels, giant clams and oysters are also types of mollusc.

ECHINODERMS

This group includes starfish and sea urchins. Echinoderms don't have heads or legs, but under their skin there is a tough shell made of minerals. Many echinoderms are circular in shape, or have five 'arms', and are covered in spines.

ARTHROPODS

About 75 per cent of known species of animal belong to this huge group. Arthropods have jointed legs and a tough outer skin called an exoskeleton. Insects, crustaceans and spiders are all types of arthropod. This is the only group of invertebrates that can fly, having evolved flight more than 100 million years before birds or reptiles.

VERTEBRATE LIFE

A VERTEBRATE IS AN ANIMAL WITH A BACKBONE AND A SKELETON. Fish, amphibians, reptiles, birds and mammals are all vertebrates. In general, vertebrates can grow bigger than invertebrates thanks to their bony skeletons, which give them strength and support without becoming too heavy.

BIG BRAINS

A vertebrate's backbone protects the spinal cord, which carries information between the body and the brain. Protected by a bony skull, the brain controls how the animal reacts to the world around it and allows vertebrate animals to behave in complex ways. As a result many species show signs of considerable intelligence.

Shortfin makos are the fastest sharks in the world. Adults are 2 to 4 metres long and give birth to up to 25 young, called pups, at a time.

FISH

Scientists have discovered and named about 34,000 species of fish so far, but there are probably plenty more lurking in the ocean's dark depths. Most fish have streamlined bodies that are covered in scales. They use gills to breathe in water. There are two main groups of fish – those with bony skeletons and those that have skeletons made from a bony substance called cartilage, which is bendier than normal bone.

SHARKS

Sharks are fish that have skeletons made from cartilage. The scales on their skin are strengthened with enamel – the same hard substance that makes our teeth strong. All sharks are predators and some of them combine superb senses with great speeds to find, hunt and catch their prey. Others are camouflaged and spend their lives on the seabed, preferring to hunt with stealth.

Seahorses are weak swimmers and wrap their curly tails around seaweed or coral to avoid being swept away by sea currents.

BONY FISH

Most fish have skeletons made of bone, not cartilage. They exist in a huge range of sizes, shapes and habitats. Some of the smallest vertebrates in world are tiny bony fish that are less than 1 centimetre long, but oarfish can grow to more than 7 metres long!

REPTILES AND AMPHIBIANS

THE FIRST REPTILES EVOLVED FROM AMPHIBIANS, BUT THESE TWO GROUPS OF VERTEBRATES NOW OFTEN INHABIT VERY DIFFERENT PLACES. Reptiles prefer hot, dry habitats while most amphibians prefer cooler, moister homes. Neither group has been particularly successful at settling in the world's coldest regions.

AMPHIBIANS

Frogs, toads, salamanders and newts are types of amphibian. Most begin their life as a legless tadpole in water after hatching from soft eggs. As the tadpoles mature they lose their tails, grow lungs and limbs and are able to live on land.

Many amphibians have moist skin.

REPTILES

Crocodiles, snakes, lizards and tortoises are all types of reptile. They have scaly skin and most of them lay eggs, although some species of snake and lizard give birth to live young. Reptiles were the first vertebrates to spend their whole lives on land. They were the dominant animals during the Age of the Dinosaurs, until the mammals took over.

Giant tortoises are protected by scales of keratin that create a shell structure.

COLD-BLOODED CREATURES

Reptiles and amphibians are often described as cold-blooded. Unlike birds and mammals, they cannot control the temperature of their body. This means that when they are cold they need to move into the sunlight to warm up, and when they are hot they move into the shade to cool down.

Many reptiles have colourful or patterned skin — chameleons can even change colour.

DEADLY VENOM

Some reptiles and amphibians evolved the ability to use poisons to kill their prey or to defend themselves. Most snakes and some lizards use their teeth to inject their poison, called venom. Many amphibians produce a toxic slime on their skin. Poison-arrow frogs are coated in a slime so deadly that they can kill a mammal with just one touch.

Every blue poison arrow frog has its own pattern of black spots.

BIG AND SMALL

Most amphibians are small. Reptiles, however, have been able to achieve far greater sizes. The long-necked sauropod dinosaurs could reach lengths of 30 metres or more. Today the largest reptiles are saltwater crocodiles at around 5 metres and reticulated pythons that can grow to more than 6 metres long.

Pythons are large snakes that squeeze their prey to death rather than killing with venom.

BIRDS

BIRDS ARE FEATHERED VERTEBRATES THAT LAY EGGS. They have wings, although not all birds can fly. The first birds evolved when dinosaurs ruled the Earth, around 150 million years ago and today there are about 10,300 species. Birds have made their homes all across the globe, from islands to mountain-tops – and almost everywhere in between!

BIRD BODY BASICS

A bird's skeleton needs to be both strong and lightweight, so it has many tiny holes in it, like a sponge. The forelimbs are adapted for flying and the hind limbs have clawed toes for gripping and perching. A bird's toothless mouth is called a beak, or bill, and the size and shape of its beak is perfect for the bird's diet.

PARROTS

Although many birds can sing, parrots and their relatives are particularly impressive, with many species able to copy, or mimic, the sounds they hear. These birds are very noisy, colourful and use their hooked beak to eat fruit, seeds and nuts, while skilfully gripping on to the food with their long toes.

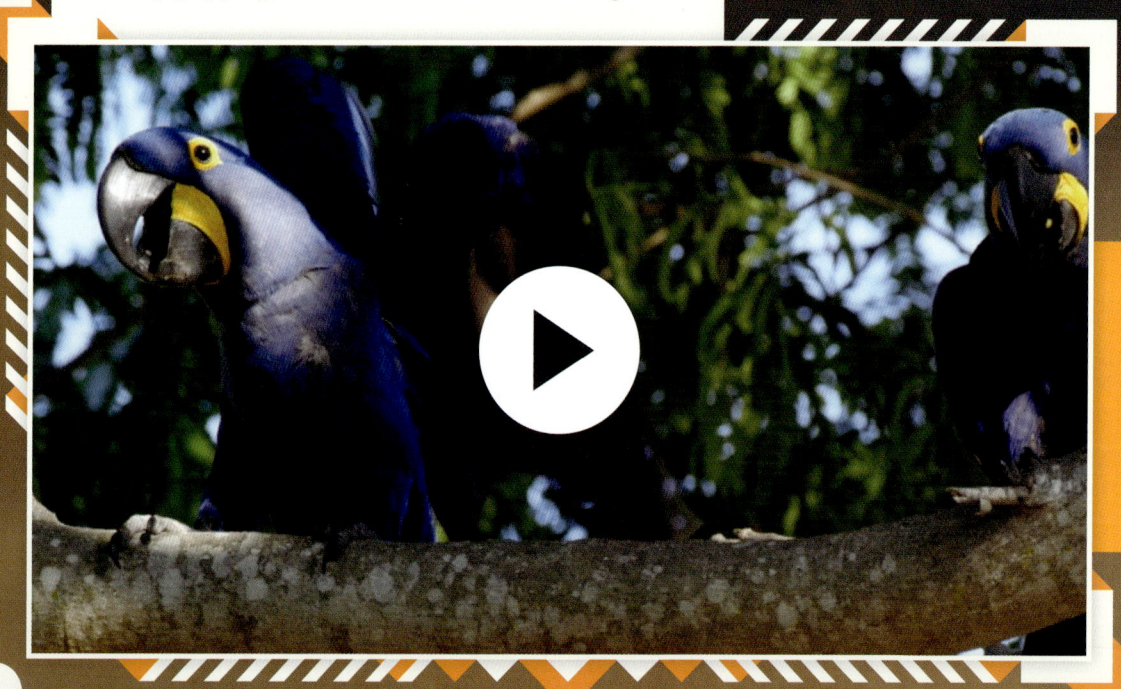

Wing

Beak

Talons

Tail

Most birds need trees to survive. A tree is a good place to hide from predators, find food and build a nest. When trees are cut down, birds and many other animals can lose their home.

PERCHING BIRDS

The largest group of birds are the perching birds, or passerines. They are mostly small and have evolved feet for gripping on to twigs, so these birds are common in woodland habitats around the world.

BIRDS OF PREY

Birds of prey, or raptors, are amongst the most powerful of all birds. They have a strong, curved beak for killing their prey and large clawed feet called talons. Birds of prey have superb eyesight for spotting prey from a great distance.

OWLS

Owls are mostly nocturnal birds with superb senses of sight and hearing. Many species have soft, fluffy feathers on their wingtips and feet to help muffle the sound as they swoop close to the ground.

FLIGHTLESS BIRDS

Many of the largest birds have lost the ability to fly and often rely on their size or speed to survive. Ostriches, emus and cassowaries are all large, flightless birds. Penguins use their wings like flippers to fly through the water, chasing fish in the cooler oceans around the Antarctic.

King penguins dive more than 100 metres underwater in search of fish to eat.

WATER BIRDS

Many birds soar above the seas, searching for marine creatures to pluck from the water. Other types of water bird, such as flamingos, wade along the shoreline, picking shellfish and worms from the mud and sand. Rivers and lakes are also a good source of food for many birds.

MAMMALS

MAMMALS ARE VERTEBRATES THAT HAVE FUR AND FEED THEIR YOUNG WITH MILK. The first mammals walked on land, but many species evolved to live in water, and bats evolved as the only true flying mammal. Scientists have found and named about 5,800 species of mammal, but about one-third of them are now threatened with extinction.

EGGS AND POUCHES

Most mammals give birth to their young but monotremes, such as the duck-billed platypus and echidna, are unusual mammals that lay eggs instead.

Marsupials are mammals that give birth to tiny young that are raised in a pouch on the mother's body. Kangaroos, koalas, wombats and opossums are all marsupials.

A koala mother carries her young, which is called a joey.

BATS

Most bats are nocturnal and hunt insects at night, using echolocation. They create sounds that bounce off objects nearby, such as flying bugs or trees. The bats use the echoes of the sounds to work out the size and location of their prey. Fruit-eating bats are larger and use excellent senses of smell and sight to find food.

PRIMATES

Monkeys, apes, lemurs and tamarins are all types of primate. Primates are adapted for living in trees, so their future is threatened by the loss of forests around the world. A primate has forward-facing eyes, long, slender limbs for climbing and hands for gripping.

Squirrel monkeys live in the forests of South and Central America.

WATER MAMMALS

Whales, dolphins, seals, sea lions, otters and manatees are mammals that are superbly adapted for a life in water. They are all good swimmers and can spend time underwater, but they have lungs which means they must return to the surface to breathe.

Whale mothers keep their young very close and help push them to the surface of the water so they can breathe.

CATS AND DOGS

Wild members of the cat family (felids) and dog family (canids) are intelligent predators that use strategies to find, hunt and kill their prey. They are equipped with sharp teeth, incredible senses, speed and strength. Some types, such as wolves and lions, work in groups to share the work of chasing and catching a fast-moving animal. Many canids and felids are at risk of extinction after being hunted by humans, or because their habitats have been destroyed.

Male deer grow large bony horns called antlers on their heads. They use them to fight.

GRAZERS

Many mammals rely on a diet of plants to sustain themselves, and spend most of the day grazing. Elephants and giraffes use their great size to strip leaves and bark from trees. Deer, antelope, cattle and members of the horse family (equids) often live in herds so they can share the job of looking out for predators as they eat.

Rodents, rabbits and other small grazing mammals are found all around the world. They can make their homes in a wide variety of habitats, from deserts to riverbanks, but many of them are also able to live alongside humans in gardens, towns and cities.

HOW ANIMALS LIVE

ANIMALS ARE THE MOST VARIED ORGANISMS ON EARTH. They show a huge range in body structure and way of life. Nevertheless, they all need to be able to carry out certain processes. These include feeding, moving, breathing and sensing the world around them.

MOVING

Animals can fly, swim, walk, crawl, run, climb and even slither. Most of them rely on a system of muscles to power their movement. Some creatures are able to travel across the globe in search of food or mates, but others stay in one place, and wait for food to come to them.

BREATHING

When animals breathe they take in air so they can extract the oxygen they need to release energy from food. While many animals can absorb oxygen through their skin, others have special organs, such as gills and lungs, to do this important job. Waste gases are expelled from the body when they breathe out.

All spiders breathe air. Water spiders survive in ponds by carrying a bubble of air.

Hummingbirds can hover at a flower and use their long beaks to suck nectar, which is rich in sugar and energy.

FEEDING

Finding and eating food uses a lot of an animal's energy and time, and it can put them at risk of being caught and killed by predators. Animals that eat a diet of plants are called herbivores, and those that eat meat are carnivores. Scavengers are nature's cleaners because they eat dead animals or plants that they find.

SENSES

An animal uses its senses to get information about the world around it. This information is used by the animal to find food and mates, care for its young, stay safe and move through its environment. The five key senses are: sight, hearing, touch, taste and smell.

Most owls hunt at night using superb senses of hearing and sight to find prey.

LIFE CYCLES

MOST ANIMALS BEGIN THEIR LIVES AS EGGS AND THEY GROW AND CHANGE AS THEY GET OLDER. They reach an age when they are mature enough to reproduce, or have their own young, and eventually die. The story of how an animal passes through these life stages is called a life cycle.

COURTSHIP AND MATING

When it is time to reproduce, animals need to find a mate. In many species the females choose the mate, so males compete to impress them. Sometimes they fight each other to win a female's attention, or they dance (like the lyrebird above) or sing to show a female that they are healthy and strong enough to be a good mate.

COMMUNICATION

Animals have many ways to communicate with each other. Chameleons, for example, can change the colour of their skin to show they are feeling threatened or are interested in mating, and elephants flap their ears to show anger. Bees use special dances to tell each other where to find flowers and ants use chemicals to warn of danger.

CARING FOR THE YOUNG

Most animals begin life as eggs that have been laid by the mother, but others are kept protected inside the mother's body until they are big enough to be born. Some mothers produce hundreds, even thousands, of eggs at a time and take no care of the eggs once they have been laid. At the other end of the scale, there are mothers who give birth to one baby at a time and spend years raising it to adulthood. In some species, especially birds and mammals, fathers share in the care of their young.

Wolf spiders carry their babies on their back.

LIVING IN GROUPS

Living and working together can help animals in the battle for survival. While some creatures live together as small families, others form large groups. They can share the work of finding food, building their homes and looking out for predators. Meerkats, for example, live in large family groups called mobs. They work together to dig burrows where they live and take it in turns to guard the entrances. Older meerkats teach their young how to spot predators and kill scorpions safely, removing the venomous sting before eating them.

An orangutan mother has one baby at a time and cares for it until it is about seven years old. She uses that time to teach it how and where to find food.

MIGRATING

Animals migrate, or travel long distances, to find food, mates or rear their young. These migrations can be an essential part of a species' life cycle, but human activities can make migrations increasingly difficult in the modern world. Christmas Island red crabs, for example, migrate every year from forests to the coast to breed, but they now struggle to make their journeys because they are in danger of being crushed by cars when crossing the roads along their routes.

3 HABITATS

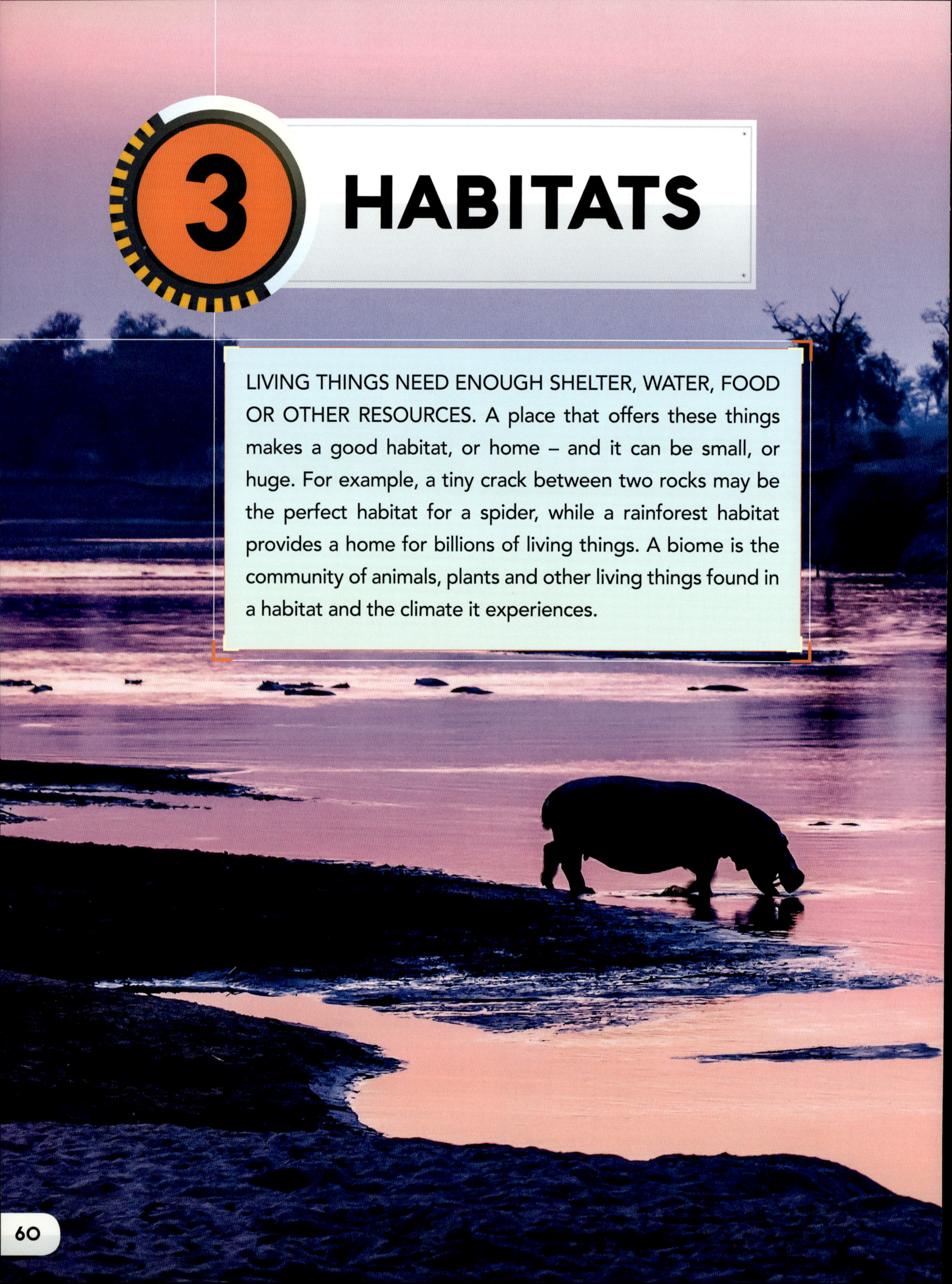

LIVING THINGS NEED ENOUGH SHELTER, WATER, FOOD OR OTHER RESOURCES. A place that offers these things makes a good habitat, or home – and it can be small, or huge. For example, a tiny crack between two rocks may be the perfect habitat for a spider, while a rainforest habitat provides a home for billions of living things. A biome is the community of animals, plants and other living things found in a habitat and the climate it experiences.

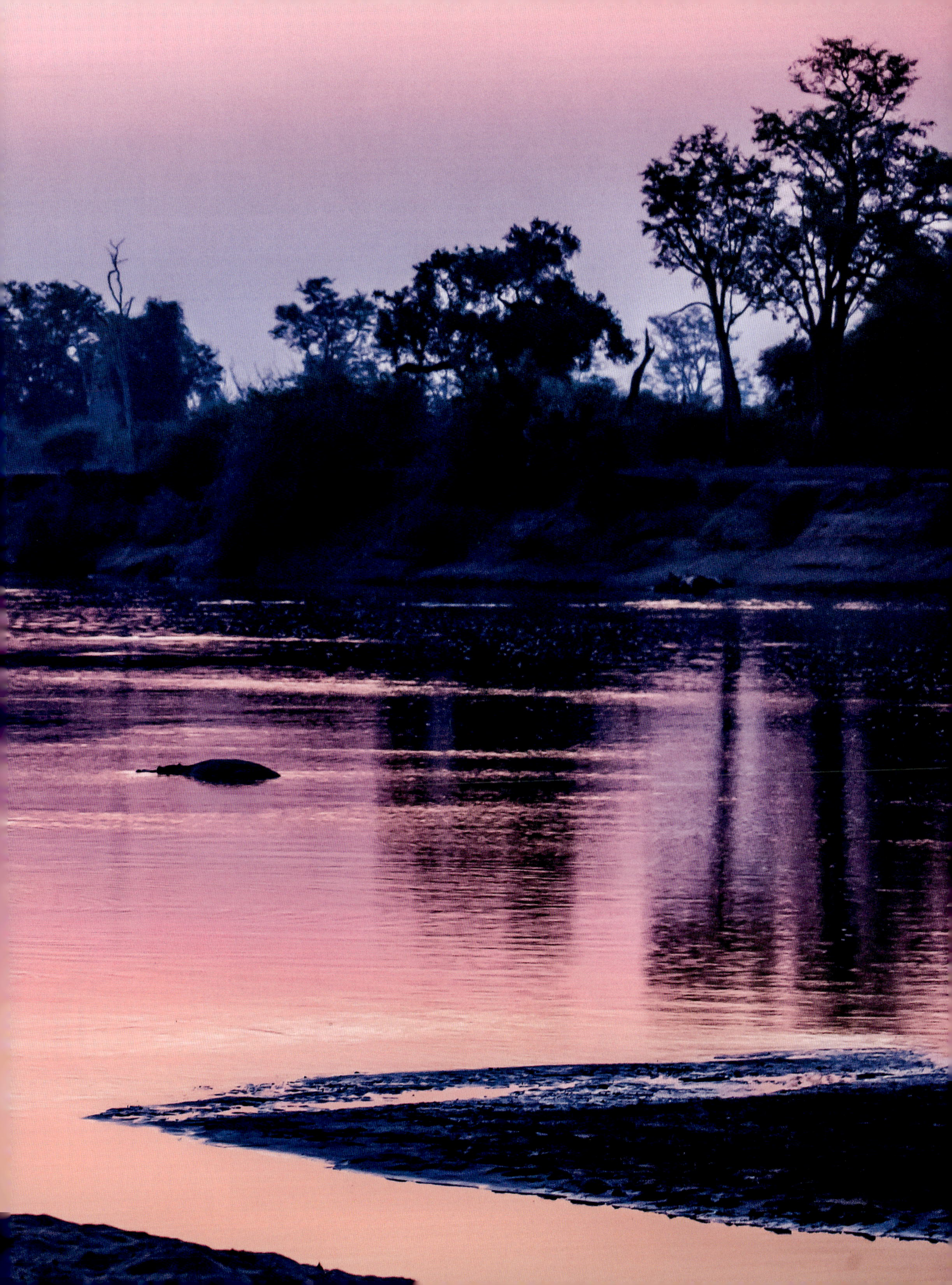

THE POLAR BIOME

THE POLES ARE TWO OF THE MOST EXTREME PLACES ON EARTH. The temperature is often far below zero, creating frozen wildernesses where only the toughest animals and plants can survive. The Arctic is a frozen ocean that spans the North Pole and the Antarctic is an icy continent that covers the South Pole.

LIFE ON ICE

The winters are long and harsh in the polar biome, and the days are short. Icy winds whip across the landscape, and blizzards smother the land with snow, so few plants manage to live here. Summers are very short, and even though the sun shines, it rarely lifts the temperature much above freezing.

POLAR PENGUINS

Most penguins prefer to live in cold places, and can even overheat when the weather warms up! These flightless birds use their flipper-like wings to swim through the sea at great speeds, chasing fish. Adélie penguins spend the winter on Antarctica where they breed. They can reach speeds of around 15 kilometres an hour when hunting or fleeing from predators underwater.

The treeless land around the Arctic Ocean is called the tundra, and it is frozen for much of the year. In spring, the land thaws briefly, and plants burst into life.

SEALS AND WHALES

Seals and whales are mammals but they are adapted for a life at sea, with thick layers of blubber and a body shape that is perfect for swimming. Seals return to land to give birth and rest, but whales spend their whole lives in water. They breathe through nostrils on the top of their heads, called blowholes.

Harp seal pups are white to blend into the snow. Their fur changes to a silvery-grey colour as they grow older.

POLAR ICE IN PERIL

Scientists have discovered that the polar ice is melting, and the Artic and Antarctic habitats are changing. This threatens the future of the animals that live there. However, it is likely to have other important consequences for the rest of the world too, as the melt-water is causing the sea level to rise.

POLAR BEARS

Like other animals of the Arctic and Antarctic, the polar bear is suited to a life in the cold. A thick coat of fur and a layer of fat keeps it warm. Its white colour helps to camouflage this huge predator as it lies by a seal's breathing hole, waiting to pounce. Polar bear mothers spend the worst winter months in a snow den, caring for their cubs and waiting for the spring to arrive.

TEMPERATE FORESTS

SOUTH OF THE ARCTIC THERE ARE VAST AREAS OF LAND THAT EXPERIENCE A MILDER CLIMATE AND WARMER TEMPERATURES. This is called the temperate zone and it is a place where forests grow well. A forest makes a good habitat for many animals as it offers plenty of food and places to shelter from both weather and predators.

THE TAIGA

South of the Arctic tundra the land is blanketed in trees that can cope with harsh winters. This is the boreal forest, or taiga. In Russia the boreal forest stretches for more than 1,500 kilometres and in North America it covers one-quarter of the continent. Conifer trees dominate the boreal forest because they can cope with heavy snowfalls, which slip off the sloping branches without damaging them.

Wolverines and other predators of the boreal forest are not fussy eaters. They hunt almost any animal they can catch, and often feed on carrion too.

WOLVES, TIGERS AND BEARS

For many thousands of years the temperate forests have been home to large predators such as wolves, tigers and bears. Today their numbers have all declined because humans have moved into these areas to hunt animals or cut down trees. The wood from conifer trees is used for building and making paper products, but the trees are also removed to make room for roads and towns.

Animals, like the European badger, find shelter in or below an oak tree and feed on the flowers, leaves and acorns.

THE MIGHTY OAK

There are about 600 species of oak tree and they grow in woodlands north of the Equator. They live for 800 years or more and grow acorns that are food for many animals. Oaks are often called a 'keystone species' because they support a large range of animals, plants and fungi that rely on them to survive.

BROAD-LEAVED FORESTS

Conifers are trees that keep their leaves all year round, but broad-leaved trees lose their leaves in the autumn. They are described as deciduous trees and they most commonly grow in places that are warmer than the boreal forest. The fallen leaves collect on the forest floor, creating an entirely new biome where bugs and fungi can shelter.

GRASSLANDS

GRASSLANDS GROW IN PLACES WHERE THERE IS NOT ENOUGH RAIN FOR FORESTS BUT THERE IS TOO MUCH RAIN FOR DESERTS TO DEVELOP. They are found in temperate zones, as well as in the warmer tropical areas. In Africa, grasslands are called the savannah. In the Americas they are known as prairies or pampas, and in Eurasia they are called the steppe.

TOUGH GRASS

Grass is a survivor. It can cope with long periods of drought and bursts into life after a rainfall, growing long green blades of leaf at great speed. Unlike most plants, grass can survive even after being burned or nibbled to the ground, so it has become the main food for grazing animals all over the world.

SAVANNAH

African grasslands are home to herbivores, such as elephants, giraffes, hippos and rhinoceroses, as well as large herds of antelope. Many savannah animals follow the seasonal rains as they fall across the plains, bringing life to areas after months of drought, often forming waterholes where many animals gather to drink.

GRAN CHACO

The Gran Chaco is an area of pampas and woodland in South America. It is hot and dry in the summer but after heavy rainfall the rivers flood, creating wetlands and swamps. It is one of the world's most precious habitats but Gran Chaco has been threatened by human activity such as farming and road-building.

Armadillos are strange-looking mammals that live in the Gran Chaco. They have bony plates on their body for protection from predators, and eat grubs.

PRAIRIE DOGS

A prairie dog is a burrowing rodent that lives in huge groups underground. A prairie dog colony is called a town and the largest ones can contain millions. They are a keystone species because other animals, such as rabbits, snakes and burrowing owls also depend on their burrows for a home. They are hunted by birds of prey, black-footed ferrets and American badgers.

Prairie dogs are active in the day, so some members of the group stand watch and call loudly if they spot predators.

TROPICAL RAINFORESTS

TROPICAL RAINFORESTS ARE HOT, HUMID HABITATS, WHICH TEEM WITH THE SIGHTS AND SOUNDS OF LIFE. Situated around the equator, rainforests stay warm and wet all year round. This provides ideal growing conditions for plants and the animals that feed on them. As such, rainforests are home to around half of the world's plant and animal species.

EMERGENT LAYER ☀ 100%

RAINFOREST LAYERS

Animals inhabit all four levels of the rainforest. It gets darker the lower you go down. The canopy is a thick layer of treetops, which is like the rainforest ceiling. A few tall 'emergent' trees poke up above the canopy. The understorey, below the canopy, is made up of small trees, shrubs and vines. Few plants grow on the dark forest floor, but it is buzzing with life, including insects and mammals.

All rainforests are made up of four layers: the emergent layer, the canopy, understorey and forest floor.

CANOPY LAYER ☀ 95%

AMAZON RAINFOREST

The Amazon is the largest rainforest in the world at around 5.5 million square kilometers wide. Leaves, fruits and nuts are the main source of food in the Amazon and consumed in large amounts by monkeys, sloths, insects and birds. Many birds feed on insects that live between the forest floor and canopy; others prefer fruit, flowers or other animals. Almost half the world's species of bird are found in the Amazon rainforest.

UNDERSTOREY LAYER ☀ 5%

FOREST FLOOR ☀ 2%

Over 80,000 acres of rainforest are cut down every day.

LOGGING THE AMAZON

The Amazon keeps its warm wet climate all year round, which provides the perfect growing conditions for its rich vegetation. Because this vegetation produces around 20 per cent of the world's oxygen, the Amazon is known as 'the lungs of the Earth'. However, the Amazon is under great threat from deforestation. This deforestation is contributing to global climate change, as rainforests help regulate toxic gases in the atmosphere.

INDONESIAN RAINFOREST

The Indonesian rainforest is spread across four of Indonesia's islands: Sumatra, Borneo, Sulawesi and New Guinea. It is the third largest rainforest in the world. In Sumatra, the rainforest is the only place where tigers, orangutans, rhinos and elephants all live together in the wild. There are also over 29,000 species of plant and new plants are discovered all the time. Over 400 new plant species have been identified here since 1995.

Orangutans live in the Indonesian rainforest and spend 90 per cent of their time in the tree tops.

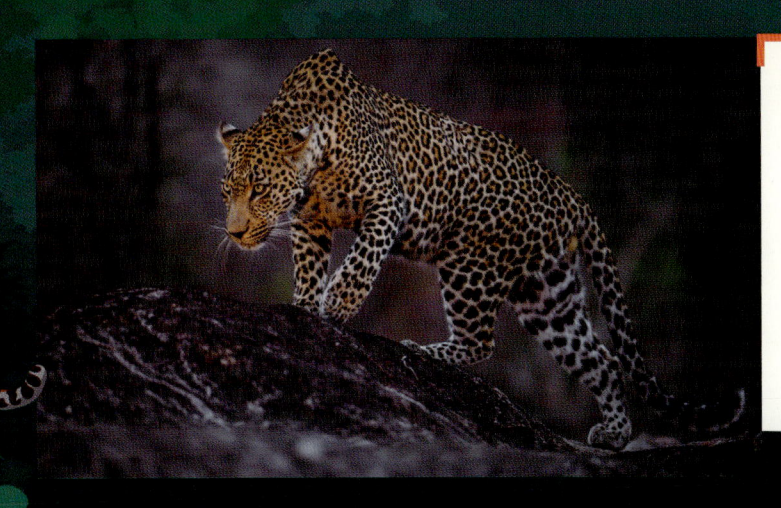

CENTRAL AFRICAN RAINFOREST

The Central African rainforest covers 2 million square kilometres of the Congo Basin and is the second largest rainforest in the world. Many large mammals live here including gorillas, leopards and forest elephants.

TROPICAL DRY FORESTS

IT RAINS MOST DAYS IN A TROPICAL RAINFOREST, BUT RAIN IS LESS FREQUENT IN A TROPICAL DRY FOREST. In some forests most of the rain comes during the monsoon season when hot, wet winds bring heavy rainfall. In other forests, especially in the southern parts of Africa and South America, there is little rain throughout the year.

MADAGASCAR

Dry forests in Madagascar have a tropical climate and a wet season that lasts from October to April. They are a precious habitat for many animals that live nowhere else on the planet. However, 97 per cent of the dry forest biome has been destroyed by humans who have cut down trees for firewood or for farmland.

The Helmet Vanga has a very distinctive, hooked blue beak. Its species is threatened due to habitat loss.

THE AYE-AYE

Lemurs are monkey-like primates that live on the island of Madagascar. The aye-aye is a small lemur that climbs through the trees at night, hunting for bugs to eat. It listens out for the sound of insects moving or buzzing and uses its long fingers to dig them out from tree bark. Other lemurs help the forest because they eat berries and fruits. The seeds pass through their bodies and fall to the forest floor where some of them can grow.

TIGER FOREST

Ranthambore is a region of India where more than 50 Bengal tigers prowl through the dense forest. On the hottest days, just before the monsoon rains arrive, they wallow in any cool pools of water they can find. At this time of year, the trees are bare and the grass has turned yellow and straw-like. The trees are resting, waiting for the rains, which can be so heavy that they flood the land. Then the forest will burst into life, and the tigers will find plenty of animals to hunt.

MOUNTAINS

THE WORLD'S TALLEST HILLS ARE CALLED MOUNTAINS AND MOST OF THEM ARE MORE THAN 2,000 METRES HIGH. Although mountains can be a challenging place to live, they are home to a wide range of animals and plants.

ON THE MOVE

There are different zones on a mountain. The low zones often have wet or mild climates where trees can grow. Further up the mountain slopes the soil becomes shallow and few trees can grow because they need deep soil for their roots. At the peak there are bare rocks with even fewer plants. While some animals make their home in just one part of a mountain, others travel between zones, especially in the colder months when they move downhill to stay out of the worst weather.

Bighorn sheep of North America are nimble animals that can leap from danger when mountain lions chase them. They are such skilled climbers they can easily move up and down the mountain, looking for plants to eat.

ECOSYSTEMS

An ecosystem is a place and all the organisms in it. It includes the conditions that make life possible, such as the climate, soil type and other environmental features. A mountain is an unusual ecosystem because its top, or peak, is at high altitude (high up above ground). There is less air at altitude and the wind can be very fierce. Although the Sun's rays are stronger, the nights can be bitterly cold and snow often forms in the winter, even on tropical mountains such as Mount Kenya.

THE HIMALAYAS

The Himalayas are the tallest mountains in the world and include Mount Everest, which is the highest point on Earth at 8,850 metres. Beyond 6,000 metres there is permanent ice and snow, so almost nothing lives beyond this point. However, some animals do manage to survive on the slopes, including shy snow leopards and the markhor goats that they hunt.

Forests in the foothills of the Himalayas are home to clouded leopards, Asian elephants, snub-nosed monkeys and Asian black bears.

VALLEYS

A valley is the area between two mountains that has usually been carved out of the rock by rivers or glaciers. These places are often lush and full of life because the water attracts many animals to them. Plants grow well in the damp soil around, especially after rivers flood and spread nutrients into the ground.

RIVERS AND WETLANDS

MOST OF THE PLANET'S FRESH WATER IS HIDDEN BENEATH THE GROUND OR FROZEN AS ICE, and less than one per cent of the total is found in rivers, lakes and wetlands. These environments are an important habitat for many animals and plants, and a source of drinking water for visiting creatures.

FRESHWATER PLANTS

The water in rivers and lakes usually has more nutrients in it than seawater, so it is a good place for plants such as reeds and water lilies to grow. The smallest plants are microscopic algae that turn the water green as they float at the surface, gathering sunlight for photosynthesis. The largest plants are trees that are able to survive with their roots permanently soaking in water.

The water hyacinth is a floating plant with purple-black trailing roots. It can grow and multiply to cover whole ponds and lakes.

THE AMAZING AMAZON

The Amazon River takes water on an incredible journey that covers 6,430 kilometres from the Andes Mountains to the Atlantic Ocean. In some places, the river is 16 kilometres wide and it pours 770 billion litres of water into the sea every hour! The Amazon Rainforest has sprung up around this source of fresh water, creating one of the world's largest and most important habitats.

LAKE BAIKAL

Lake Baikal is the oldest and deepest lake in the world. More than 33 rivers flow into it and this Russian lake holds about 20 per cent of the world's fresh water. It is home to more than 2,000 species of plants and animals, most of which live nowhere else in the world.

The Baikal seal is unusual because it spends its whole life in freshwater. They can hold their breath for up to 70 minutes!

CHANGING PLACES

Many lakes, rivers and wetlands are in danger of drying up. Farmers take fresh water from rivers to irrigate their crops, and freshwater is piped into towns for homes and businesses to use. Chemicals and sewage are types of pollution that are often poured into rivers, killing wildlife.

Polluted waterways spread diseases and damage wildlife.

RIVER ROUTES

Salmon use rivers to reach their breeding places. When it is time to mate and lay their eggs, salmon leave the sea and swim upriver to reach shallow areas where their young, or fry, are safer than they would be in the sea. After the baby salmon hatch they will be swept down the river to the sea, where they grow into adults.

As salmon go on their epic migration upriver, bears lie in wait to grab the leaping fish!

COASTS

THE COAST IS THE STRIP OF LAND THAT MEETS THE SEA AND IT IS AN EXCITING, DYNAMIC HABITAT. Waves lash the coast, breaking up the land and carving rocks into strange shapes. The tides shift huge amounts of sand and mud and flood the homes of coastal animals every high tide. It is a challenging place to live!

An oystercatcher's strong beak is a useful tool for cracking open shells.

WADERS AND DIVERS

Coasts are popular with birds – every time the tide goes out, wading birds, such as oystercatchers, stroll along the beach searching for shellfish to eat. Other birds, such as puffins, dive into the shallow water to grab fish and take them back to their cliff-top nests to feed their chicks.

Coasts offer many hiding places for ragworms and an endless supply of small prey to hunt.

MUDDY HOMES

Sand and mud make good homes for small animals such as worms and shellfish that dig into the beach. Ragworms hide in their burrows and use bristles that work like rows of tiny legs to move them through tunnels of mud. These predators have strong jaws for grabbing other small animals, but they are no match for the wading birds that snap them up.

TOURISTS AND TRASH

A steady supply of food makes coasts popular with animals that have young to feed. Coasts are also popular with people, and hotels have been built alongside many of the most beautiful beaches. The lights from these buildings can confuse baby turtles, which use moonlight to guide them back to the sea. Tourists are sometimes careless with their rubbish, which pollutes the coastline.

Turtles live in the sea but the females must clamber onto the beach to bury their eggs in the sand. When the eggs hatch the baby turtles must find their way back to the water.

ROCK POOLS

On some coasts, pools remain flooded with seawater even when the tide is out. These rock pools are often filled with animals, from spiny sea urchins to sea anemones, crabs and little fish. Seaweeds don't have roots, but they can stick themselves to rocky surfaces.

SHALLOW WATER

SHALLOW SEAWATER SURROUNDS THE LAND. It is warmer than the deep water that lies beyond and full of life. There are animals and plants that live here all year round, and others that visit to breed and feed. One of the most incredible sights in shallow water is a coral reef – a type of habitat that is sometimes called the rainforest of the sea.

KELP FORESTS

Giant kelp is seaweed that can grow to more than 50 metres long. It is one of the fastest-growing plants, and one strand can grow by 50 centimetres in just one day! Giant kelp forests are rare habitats but, like seagrasses and coral, they are home to a great variety of animals. Their most famous inhabitants include leafy seadragons, which are camouflaged to blend into the kelp, and furry sea otters.

SEAGRASS MEADOWS

Seagrasses are unusual flowering plants that can live underwater and form large 'meadows' where fish can hide from bigger predators and turtles can graze. Manatees and dugongs are rare sea mammals that also live among the seagrasses, which they eat.

Most seagrasses grow in water that is more than 5 metres deep, where they are always underwater and not battered by waves.

CORAL REEFS

Coral polyps are small animals that build stony cups to live in. They use their tentacles to catch food that wafts past in the currents. Over thousands of years, billions of coral polyps can build a stony reef, which becomes a home for many creatures from baby sharks to turtles and sea snakes.

Coral polyps need clean, warm and salty water to live.

THE GREAT BARRIER REEF

The Great Barrier Reef lies east of Australia and it is the world's largest coral reef. It grows in a marine park that stretches for more than 3,000 kilometres. The reef is about 65 kilometres wide, and it is the only living thing that can be seen from space. This unique habitat is home to more than 400 kinds of coral, 1500 kinds of fish and 200 types of bird.

OPEN OCEANS

THE OPEN OCEANS ARE THE LARGEST HABITAT ON EARTH. Sunlight reaches only the upper layers of water, and at depths of 1,000 metres the water turns colder and darker. Many strange animals manage to survive in this mysterious place.

200 M

1,000 M

4,000 M

6,000 M

10,000 M

80

SUNLIGHT ZONE
(0–200 metres)

Sunlight travels through the water and is gradually absorbed, so the upper part of the ocean is called the sunlight zone. This is where tiny floating animals and plants live. They are called plankton and they are at the base of the food chain, providing a huge source of food for other creatures.

THE TWILIGHT ZONE
(200–1,000 metres)

At this depth there is not enough light for photosynthesis, so plants and microalgae cannot survive. Many small animals spend the daytime hiding in this zone, and move up to the Sunlight Zone at night to feed on the plant plankton there.

THE DARK ZONE
(1,000–4,000 metres)

There is no light here and many animals either survive long periods without food, or they eat the particles of food that sink down from the water above. The weight of water above is huge and it pushes down, creating a pressure that is too great for many animals – including humans – to survive.

THE SEABED

The seabed is a vast area, coated in thick layers of mud and the remains of long-dead animals and plants. There are mountains, volcanoes and cracks in the oceanic plates where hot gases and super-heated water leaks out.

THE DEEP SEA

The deepest parts of the sea are more than 10,000 metres down from the surface, in ocean trenches. Few people have ever explored these depths so little is known about life in this habitat. The animals that have been discovered below 4,000 metres include shrimps, worms and sponges.

4 PEOPLE AND THE PLANET

EARTH IS OUR HOME, AND OUR IMPACT ON THIS PLANET IS SO GREAT IT CAN EVEN BE SEEN FROM SPACE. Long ago, our human ancestors lived in natural habitats and hunted or collected food, just as our primate cousins do today. Eventually, humans learned how to farm, keep animals and build towns. This progress has meant that most of us lead healthier, longer and more comfortable lives than the humans who came before us. However, we now know that changing the environment to suit us can cause great damage to the planet and other living things.

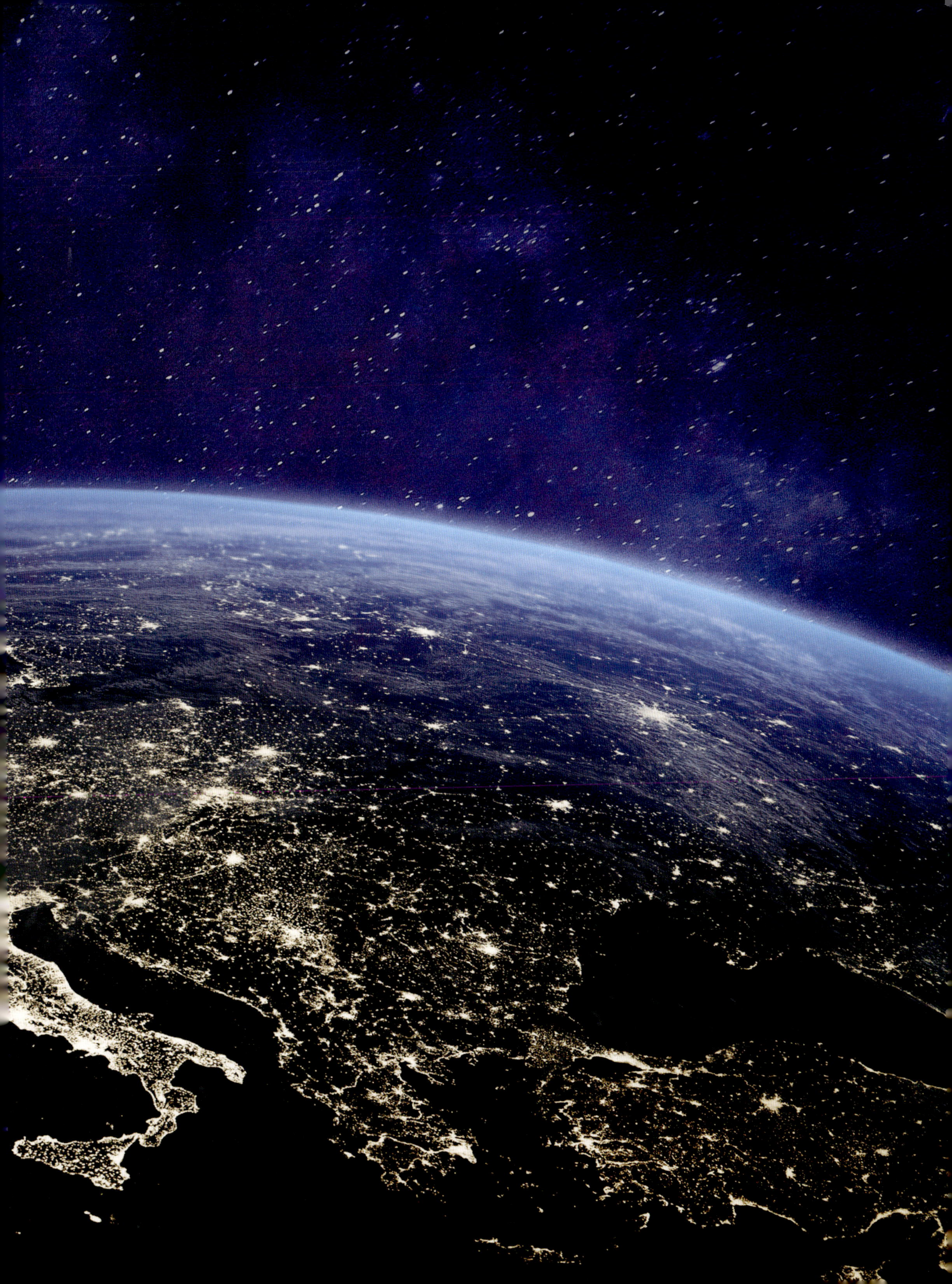

THE FIRST HUMANS

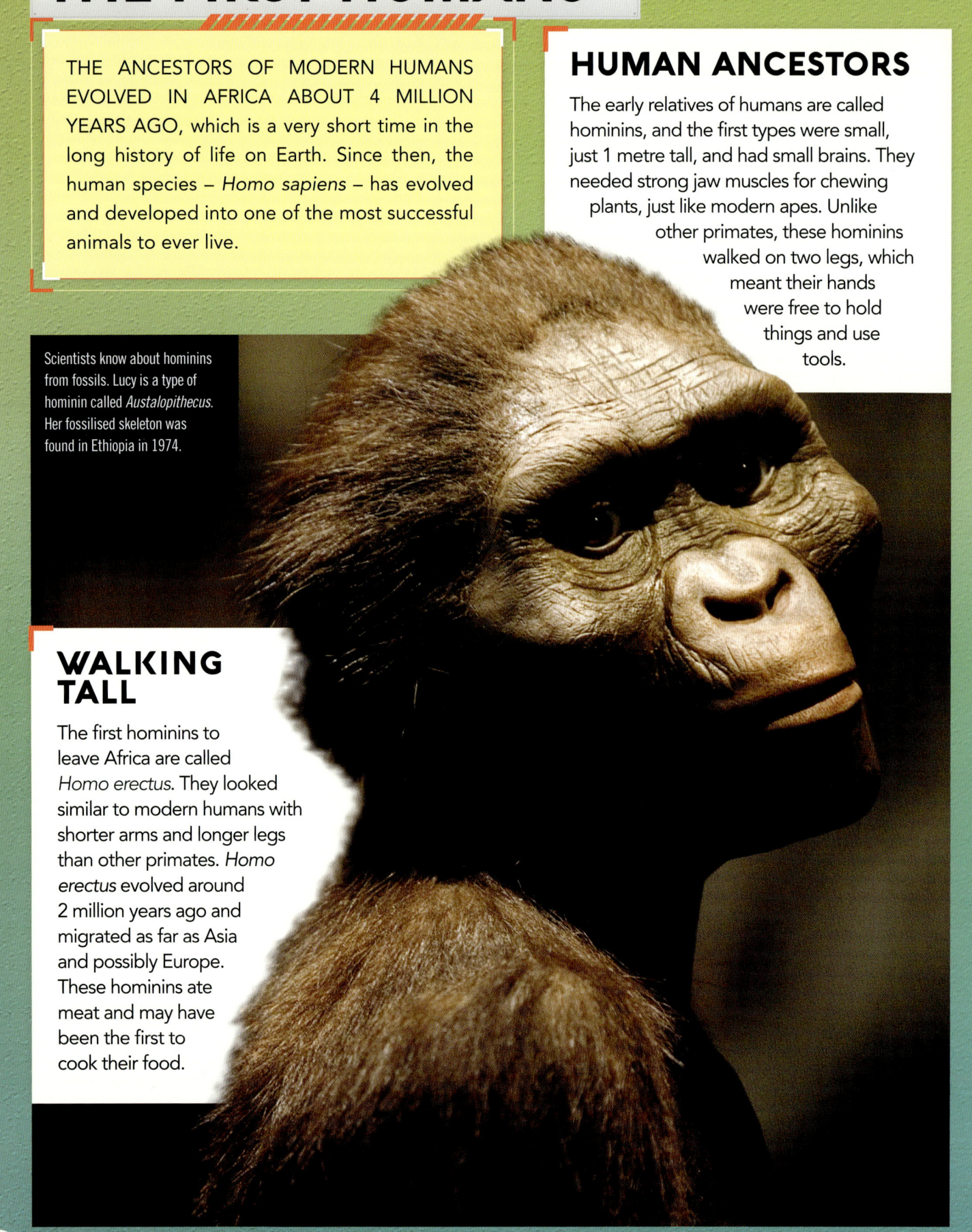

THE ANCESTORS OF MODERN HUMANS EVOLVED IN AFRICA ABOUT 4 MILLION YEARS AGO, which is a very short time in the long history of life on Earth. Since then, the human species – *Homo sapiens* – has evolved and developed into one of the most successful animals to ever live.

HUMAN ANCESTORS

The early relatives of humans are called hominins, and the first types were small, just 1 metre tall, and had small brains. They needed strong jaw muscles for chewing plants, just like modern apes. Unlike other primates, these hominins walked on two legs, which meant their hands were free to hold things and use tools.

Scientists know about hominins from fossils. Lucy is a type of hominin called *Austalopithecus*. Her fossilised skeleton was found in Ethiopia in 1974.

WALKING TALL

The first hominins to leave Africa are called *Homo erectus*. They looked similar to modern humans with shorter arms and longer legs than other primates. *Homo erectus* evolved around 2 million years ago and migrated as far as Asia and possibly Europe. These hominins ate meat and may have been the first to cook their food.

NEANDERTHALS

Neanderthals were a type of human that went extinct about 40,000 years ago. They lived in Europe and Asia while the direct ancestors of modern humans were evolving in Africa. Neanderthals were very strong and well-suited to life during a cold period called the Ice Age. They lived in groups and used stone tools to hunt large mammals together.

Neanderthals may have died out because their prey animals, such as the woolly mammoth (a distant relative of the Asian elephant) went extinct when the climate got warmer.

MODERN HUMANS

Many different types of hominin and human have evolved and so far scientists have found and named the remains of at least 22 different relatives of modern humans. Today only one species of human survives, *Homo sapiens*, which evolved in Africa about 200,000 years ago.

SECRETS OF SUCCESS

There are many reasons why modern humans have been such successful survivors. We have hands and big brains, so we are able to make things and solve problems. We can communicate well with each other, and we have created societies where we help each other and share the work that needs to be done.

HUMAN HABITATS

ONE OF THE REASONS HUMANS HAVE BEEN SUCH A SUCCESSFUL SPECIES IS OUR ABILITY TO WORK TOGETHER. That skill means we are able to survive almost anywhere on land. The first cities were built more than 8,500 years ago and today humans have made their homes on every continent except Antarctica.

STRONG SURVIVORS

The key to survival is the ability to adapt and change to suit new environments. Humans have taken this survival skill to a new level – they are able to adapt the environment to suit them. Humans are intelligent tool-makers with the ability to talk and share ideas. These skills have helped humans to grow food, make homes, carry water and build new technologies.

INDUSTRY

An industry is the business of taking raw materials, such as metals and oil, and making new things from them in factories. In the last few hundred years humans have developed an incredible range of industries. The development of industry began in Europe but has now spread over the world.

Almost everything around you is made in factories, from clothes and phones to cars and kitchen equipment.

A huge mountain of rubbish has grown alongside the Indian city of Delhi and releases toxic gases that harm the people who live nearby.

CREATING WASTE

When people build cities and factories they produce harmful waste in large amounts, which is known as pollution. Polluting gases are released when fossil fuels, such as oil, coal and gas, are burned as a source of energy. These gases enter the atmosphere and contribute to global climate change. Other forms of pollution include industrial waste, sewage and littering.

CITIES AND WILDLIFE

Urban areas are places where people have built settlements, such as cities. Some cities contain more people than entire countries! When humans build settlements they take over wild habitats where animals and plants live. This can cause great devastation and even extinctions of some species. Many animals and plants, however, adapt to the new environment and can live alongside humans.

FEEDING THE WORLD

IN 2019, THE WORLD CELEBRATED THE ANNIVERSARY OF THE FIRST MOON LANDING IN 1969. In just fifty years the world changed in many ways, but one of the most important changes was the number of people on the planet. When Neil Armstrong took his first steps on the Moon there were 3.61 billion people alive back on Earth, but 50 years later that number had more than doubled to 7.7 billion.

GROWING FOOD

Feeding a fast-growing population is an enormous challenge to the planet and its people. The first farmers grew just what their families needed, but now farming has become a huge industry, and food is transported thousands of miles to reach customers. This has many impacts on the environment.

Cows are farmed for food and milk. They release large amounts of greenhouse gases when they digest their food, contributing to global warming.

MAKING DESERTS

Fertile land can be ruined by farming and drought. It turns to desert, where few living things can survive. It has been estimated that 70 per cent of grasslands and forests are in danger of turning into deserts because of human activity.

PLANTATIONS

A plantation is a large area of farmland that grows just one crop, such as coffee, tea, sugar and palm trees. The oil from palm trees is used in many products including cakes and animal feed. Forests are often destroyed so plantations can be grown and palm oil plantations have replaced large areas of natural forests in Borneo and Sumatra, where orangutans once lived.

CHANGING NATURE

Farming and fishing are necessary to feed people, but it changes nature by destroying or damaging natural habitats. As humans have explored the world and settled into new places they have taken their domestic animals with them, and this can have a damaging effect on the local wildlife.

Humans breed domestic animals to produce ones that are more useful to them. Farm chickens look very different to their wild relative, the jungle-fowl.

WATER FOR FARMING

Farmers need water for their crops and animals. Much of this water is taken from nearby habitats, which can leave wildlife without a source of water. The Aral Sea, for example, was once the fourth largest lake in the world. It dried up after farmers piped the water to irrigate their cotton crops, leaving local people and wildlife devastated.

Growing rice requires a large amount of water. The fields also release methane, a greenhouse gas.

CHANGING THE PLANET

EARTH HAS BEEN CHANGING EVER SINCE IT FIRST EMERGED FROM THE BIG BANG AS PART OF A NEW SOLAR SYSTEM. It will continue to change until the Sun begins to run out of energy, in about 5 billion years' time. We cannot control those events, but we can control our impact on the planet.

CLIMATE CHANGE

One of the most significant changes we have made to our planet is global warming. Although the Earth has gone through many changes to its atmosphere and climate, we are altering it in a new way.

We release greenhouse gases when we burn fossil fuels to run cars, heat our homes, or provide energy for factories. These gases trap heat close to the Earth and raise the temperature, which affects climate and causes devastating floods, hurricanes and forest fires.

You can help the environment by picking up litter from beaches.

OCEANS IN TROUBLE

As the world warms, the oceans are heating up too. The ice caps around the North and South Pole are melting, releasing more water into the sea. This raises the sea level around the world, flooding coastal areas where people and wildlife live. The whole ecosystem is affected, and both land and marine creatures die.

HABITAT LOSS

Clearing land for roads, homes and factories and mining for raw materials, such as the minerals used in mobile phones, means that wildlife habitats are lost forever. Global warming changes the climate, so it is also affecting habitats. Animals and plants that live there may not have time to adapt so more species than ever are threatened with extinction.

POLLUTION

Dirty air, chemicals, sewage and garbage are all types of pollution. Plastic is a great invention, but when it is not disposed of carefully it can pollute the environment and may have a long-term effect on animal and human health. Plastic bags have even been found in the deepest parts of the Pacific Ocean.

LOOKING AHEAD

THE PLANET MAY FACE AN UNCERTAIN FUTURE, but we can make a difference when we work together to make positive changes in our lifestyles. Our precious, living planet deserves the very best of our efforts.

GO GREEN

One of the best ways to cut greenhouse gases is to turn the world green again – by planting more trees! They naturally soak up the dangerous carbon dioxide we have put in the air, and provide a home for wildlife too.

Green sources of energy do not produce greenhouse gases, so they are better for the environment. Solar, geothermal, wind and tidal energy are all alternatives to fossil fuels. One of the easiest ways to cut greenhouse gases is to use less energy by turning down the heating, turning off lights when not in use, and walking or using public transport instead of cars.

CHOOSING FOOD

Some types of fish, such as cod, have been driven close to extinction because too many have been taken from the sea to feed us. In the future, people will need to think more carefully about how and where their food is produced, and choose foods that are better for the environment.

People can volunteer to help care for rescued orangutans that have lost their homes due to deforestation.

CONSERVATION

Protecting habitats and the animals that live in them is called conservation. Taking care of the green spaces around us is one way to conserve the natural world.

Coral reefs near Mexico have been damaged. Conservationists have put statues in the water to encourage new coral polyps to settle there and help new reefs to grow.

RECYCLING

Reducing the amount of rubbish we make, or throw away, can really help save energy and reduce pollution. When you shop, look for products that use less packaging. Always recycle your waste, when you can, and dispose of your litter safely in bins.

GLOSSARY

Adaptation The way in which plants and animals gradually change to become better suited to their environment.

Algae A large group of organisms that includes simple plants, or plant-like organisms, without roots and true leaves. The group includes seaweeds.

Amphibian A group of cold-blooded vertebrates that includes frogs and toads. Most young amphibians live in water while the adults live on land.

Atmosphere The blanket of gases surrounding the Earth.

Biodiversity The variety of plant and animal life in the world or in a particular habitat.

Biome The climate and all the living things of one habitat.

Carbon dioxide A colourless and odourless gas that humans and animals breathe out. It is also formed by burning fuels, and the decomposition of animal and plant matter.

Carnivore An animal that eats other animals.

Classification The system that sorts all living things into defined groups, such as kingdoms and species.

Climate change Any significant long-term change in the typical weather conditions of a region, or the whole Earth.

Climate The typical weather conditions in an area.

Cold-blooded Relating to animals whose body temperature varies with the environment they live in, e.g. reptiles and amphibians).

Conservation Protection and preservation of the natural environment and of wildlife.

Continent A very large area of land, such as Africa or Asia.

Convergent boundary The boundary where two tectonic plates collide, causing massive earth movements, forming mountains and volcanoes.

Currents The non-stop movement of water.

Decomposition The decay of organic matter (plants and animals).

Deforestation The clearing of areas of forests and woodlands for farming or building.

Desertification The forming of a desert.

Divergent boundary The boundary where two tectonic plates are moving away from each other. Magma rises to the Earth's surface between the plates to form new crust.

Ecosystem The relationship between plants and animals and the environment they live in.

Endangered A species of plant or animal that is in danger of becoming extinct because of major threats to its habitat or because only a few of its type remain.

Environment The surroundings or living space of an animal or plant.

Erosion The process in which the Earth's surface (rocks or soil) is worn away by the effects of weather, water or ice.

Evolution The process by which living things change and develop over time to cope with a changing environment.

Exoskeleton A rigid bone-like external covering for the body in some invertebrate animals.

Extinction A species of plant or animal that has died out (is no longer in existence).

Fauna The animals of a particular region or habitat.

Flora The plants of a particular region or habitat.

Fossil fuels Natural fuels, such as oil, coal or gas, that were formed long ago from the remains of dead animals or plants.

Global warming A gradual increase in the average temperature of Earth's atmosphere.

Gravity The force that pushes and pulls on objects.

Greenhouse effect The trapping of the Sun's heat by the atmosphere. The greenhouse effect is increased by greenhouse gases, such as carbon dioxide and methane.

Habitat The natural home or environment of an animal or plant.

Herbivore An animal that only eats plants.

Invertebrates Animals that don't have backbones, e.g. insects, molluscs, spiders, worms, jellyfish, corals, crabs, squids.

Kingdoms The groups into which all living organisms are divided, to help us understand how they are related to each other and how they evolved.

Lava Magma that flows onto the Earth's surface from a volcano or crack in the crust, and which then cools and hardens into rock.

Magma A hot liquid within the Earth's crust.

Mammal: An animal that gives birth to its young and feeds it with milk. Most mammals have hair or fur.

Marine: Relating to or found in the sea.

Mesosoic Era The time from about 228 to 66 million years ago. It includes the Triassic, Jurassic and Cretaceous Periods.

Microclimate The climate of a small area, especially when this is different from the climate of the surrounding area.

Microscopic Something that is so small it can only be seen with a microscope is described as microscopic.

Migration The seasonal movement of animals from one place to another, usually to find food or water, or to reach a good place for reproduction.

Mineral A solid, natural substance that is found in rocks.

Omnivore An animal that eats both animals and plants.

Orbit The continuous movement of an object around a star or planet.

Organism A living thing, such as a plant, animal, fungus or bacteria.

Oxygen A colourless and odourless gas that animals breathe in, and which makes up about 20 per cent of the Earth's atmosphere.

Photosynthesis The process used by plants to make food from sunlight, air and water.

Polar The regions around the North and South Poles are described as polar.

Pollution Substances, such as waste or toxic gases, that cause damage to the environment.

Predator An animal that hunts other animals to eat.

Prey An animal that is hunted by other animals for food.

Reptile A group of cold-blooded vertebrates that have scaly skins e.g. snakes, tortoises and lizards.

Sewage Human waste and dirty water that is carried in sewer pipes. It usually comes from bathrooms and toilets.

Solar system The Sun and the planets that move around it.

Species A particular type of living thing, which can only mate with others of its own kind e.g. Asian elephant.

Tectonic plates The plates that make up the surface of the Earth.

Temperate An area where the climate is mostly mild is described as temperate.

Tropical An area near the Equator, where the climate is mostly hot, is described as tropical.

Venom An animal poison that is usually injected into the body of a victim, mostly by teeth, stings or claws

Vertebrate An animal that has a bony skeleton, e.g. fish, birds and mammals.

Warm-blooded Relating to animals (mainly mammals and birds) which keep a constant body temperature.

Weather The day-to-day state of the atmosphere in any given place (such as wind, rain, storms and snow).

INDEX

A
Amazon
- rainforest ... 11
- river ... 11, 21

Amphibians ... 50-51
Animals ... 37, 56, 57
- breathing ... 56
- communication ... 59
- courtship and mating ... 59
- family groups ... 58
- life cycles ... 58-59
- migration ... 59
- movement ... 57
- senses ... 57

Artificial selection ... 35
Asteroids ... 6, 16
Atmosphere ... 22-23, 24
Avalanches ... 27

B, C
Bacteria ... 31, 36, 44
Big Bang ... 6
Biomes ... 24
Birds ... 52-53
Canyons ... 9, 15
Cells ... 30, 34
Classification ... 36
Climate ... 22, 24-25
Climate change ... 15, 31, 32, 33, 35, 90, 91
Coasts ... 76-77
Conservation ... 92
Continental plates ... 11, 14
- convergent boundaries ... 11
- divergent boundaries ... 10, 19

Continents ... 8, 10, 11, 14

D, E
Dinosaurs ... 11, 30, 32, 33, 35, 50, 51, 52
Deforestation ... 69, 88
DNA ... 34
Earth (structure)
- core ... 9
- crust ... 9
- mantle ... 8, 9, 10, 11

Earthquakes ... 8, 12
Equator ... 20
Erosion ... 14, 15
Evolution ... 34-35
Extinction ... 34-35

F, G
Fish ... 48
- cartilage ... 48, 49
- sharks ... 48, 49

Flowers ... 42-43
Fossil fuels ... 19, 32
Fossils ... 31, 33
Forests ... 64-65, 70-71
- Temperate forests ... 64-65
- Tropical dry forests ... 70-71

Fungi ... 37, 44-45
- moulds ... 44
- mushrooms ... 44, 45
- penicillin ... 45
- poison ... 45
- spores ... 45
- toadstools ... 44, 45

Glaciers ... 15, 17
Global Conveyor, the ... 21
Global warming ... 90, 91

Grand Canyon ... 15
Grasslands ... 66-67
Green energy sources ... 92
Greenhouse effect ... 23
Greenhouse gases ... 32, 39, 89, 90, 92

H, I
Habitats ... 14, 18, 26, 35, 36, 37, 40, 60-81
- habitat loss ... 91
- human habitats ... 86-87

Humans ... 84-85
- hominins ... 84
- *Homo erectus* ... 84
- *homo sapiens* ... 84
- Neanderthals ... 85

Insects ... 32, 33, 42, 47
Invertebrates ... 46-47
- arthropods ... 47
- cnidarians ... 46
- enchinoderms ... 47
- molluscs ... 47
- sponges ... 46
- worms ... 47

K, L, M
Kingdoms ... 36-37
Lakes ... 16, 74, 75
Lithosphere ... 8
Mammals ... 30, 54-55
- bats ... 54
- canids ... 55
- eggs ... 54
- equids ... 55
- felids ... 55
- grazers ... 55
- marsupials ... 54
- monotremes ... 54
- primates ... 54
- rodents ... 55
- water mammals ... 55

Megafauna ... 33
Meteorites ... 7, 30
Milky Way, the ... 6
Minerals ... 9, 14, 19, 31
Moon, the ... 7, 21
Mountains ... 8, 9, 10, 14, 72-73
- Andes ... 11
- Himalayas ... 73
- Mount Everest ... 73

N, O
Natural selection ... 34
Oceans ... 10, 11, 16, 17, 18-19, 20-21, 22
- Arctic Ocean ... 18
- Atlantic Ocean ... 18
- currents ... 20, 21
- Indian Ocean ... 18, 26
- Mariana Trench ... 19
- Pacific Ocean ... 18, 19
- Southern Ocean ... 18
- temperature ... 21, 91
- tides ... 21
- waves ... 15, 20
- World Ocean ... 18-19, 21
- zones ... 80, 81

P
Palaeontologists ... 31, 33
Pangaea ... 11
Planets ... 6

Plants ... 30, 37, 38-39, 40-41
- algae ... 39
- angiosperms ... 39
- Conifers ... 38
- flowering ... 39
- photosynthesis ... 36, 37, 40, 41
- prehistoric ... 32
- protists ... 36, 39, 44

Pollination ... 42
Pollution ... 23, 35
Prehistoric life ... 32-33
- Cenozeric Era ... 30
- Mesozoic Era ... 30
- Palaeozoic Era ... 30
- Proterozoic Era ... 30

R
Rainforests (tropical) ... 68-69
- Amazon rainforest ... 68
- Central African rainforest ... 69
- Congo Basin ... 69
- deforestation ... 69
- Indonesian rainforest ... 69
- rainforest layers ... 68

Recycling ... 93
Reptiles ... 30, 32, 33, 50-51
Rivers and wetlands ... 14, 15, 16, 17, 74-75
- Amazon ... 11, 21, 74
- freshwater plants ... 74
- irrigation ... 75
- Lake Baikal ... 75

Rocks ... 9, 14, 15
- igneous ... 9
- metamorphic ... 9
- sedimentary ... 9

S, T
Seasons ... 7, 24, 25
Seeds ... 42-43
Shallow water ... 78-79
- coral reefs ... 78
- Great Barrier Reef ... 78
- kelp forests ... 79
- seagrass meadows ... 79

Solar system ... 6
Species ... 28-59
Stars ... 6
Sun ... 6, 20, 21, 22, 23, 25
Tectonic plates ... 8, 10, 11, 12, 14

V, W
Valleys ... 15
Vertebrates ... 48-49
- backbone ... 48
- brain ... 48
- skeleton ... 48, 49, 52,

Volcanoes ... 9, 12-13, 22, 23, 30
- ash ... 12, 13, 23
- lava ... 9, 12, 13
- magma ... 10, 13, 16

Water ... 9, 16-17, 18, 19, 20, 21, 23
Water cycle, the ... 16-17
Weather ... 14, 22, 24-25, 26-27
- rain ... 16, 17, 24, 25
- sandstorms ... 23, 27
- tsunamis ... 12
- wind ... 9, 15, 20, 24

Wild fires ... 27